The Potential
of Educational Futures

THE NATIONAL SOCIETY
FOR THE STUDY OF EDUCATION

Series on Contemporary Educational Issues
Kenneth J. Rehage, Series Editor

The 1971 Titles

Accountability in Education, Leon M. Lessinger and Ralph W. Tyler, Editors

Farewell to Schools??? Daniel U. Levine and Robert J. Havighurst, Editors

Models for Integrated Education, Daniel U. Levine, Editor

PYGMALION Reconsidered, Janet D. Elashoff and Richard E. Snow

Reactions to Silberman's CRISIS IN THE CLASSROOM, A. Harry Passow, Editor

The 1972 Titles

Black Students in White Schools, Edgar A. Epps, Editor

Flexibility in School Programs, Willard J. Congreve and George J. Rinehart, Editors

Performance Contracting—1969-1971, James A. Mecklenburger

The Potential of Educational Futures, Michael Marien and Warren L. Ziegler, Editors

Sex Differences and Discrimination in Education, Scarvia Anderson, Editor

The National Society for the Study of Education also publishes Yearbooks which are distributed by the University of Chicago Press.

Inquiries regarding membership in the Society may be addressed to Kenneth J. Rehage, Secretary-Treasurer, 5835 Kimbark Avenue, Chicago 60637.

The Potential
of Educational Futures

edited by

Michael Marien

and

Warren L. Ziegler

Educational Policy Research Center
Syracuse University Research Corporation

Charles A. Jones Publishing Company
Worthington, Ohio

1 2 3 4 5 6 7 8 9 10 / 76 75 74 73 72

Library of Congress Catalog Card Number: 72-85888
International Standard Book Number: 0-8396-0028-3

Printed in the United States of America

Series Foreword

The Potential of Educational Futures is one of a group of five publications constituting the second set in a series prepared under the auspices of the National Society for the Study of Education. Other titles in this second set of paperbacks dealing with "Contemporary Educational Issues" are:

Performance Contracting—1969-1971, by James Mecklenburger

Sex Differences and Discrimination in Education, edited by Scarvia B. Anderson

Flexibility in School Programs, edited by Willard J. Congreve and George J. Rinehart

Black Students in White Schools, edited by Edgar G. Epps

The response to the first set of five paperbacks in this series, published in 1971, has been very encouraging. Like their predecessors the current volumes, all dealing with timely and significant issues in education, present a useful background and analysis for those who seek a deeper understanding of some of the critical educational problems of our times.

Michael Marien and Warren L. Ziegler direct attention in this volume to the growing concern for providing a "futures-perspective" to educational planning and policy-making. They have assembled a collection of original essays by persons who have been deeply involved in efforts to apply a futures-perspective to educational problems in a variety of contexts—global, national, state, and local. While the authors stress the value, indeed the necessity of incorporating futurist thinking into considerations of educational issues, they also emphasize the difficulties of doing so in a disciplined way.

The Society wishes to express its appreciation to Messrs. Marien and Ziegler, as well as to the other "futurists" who have contributed the thoughtful essays contained in this stimulating volume.

Kenneth J. Rehage
for the Committee on the Expanded Publication
Program of the National Society for the Study of Education

The Charles A. Jones Publishing Company

International Series in Education

Adams, *Simulation Games*
Allen, Barnes, Reece, Roberson, *Teacher Self-Appraisal: A Way of Looking Over Your Own Shoulder*
Armstrong, Cornell, Kraner, Roberson, *The Development and Evaluation of Behavioral Objectives*
Braun, Edwards, *History and Theory of Early Childhood Education*
Carlton, Goodwin, *The Collective Dilemma: Negotiations in Education*
Criscuolo, *Improving Classroom Reading Instruction*
Crosswhite, Higgins, Osborne, Shumway, *Mathematics Teaching: Psychological Foundations*
Denues, *Career Perspective: Your Choice of Work*
DeStefano, *Language, Society, and Education: A Profile of Black English*
Doll, *Leadership to Improve Schools*
Drier, *K-12 Guide for Integrating Career Development into Local Curriculum*
Foster, Fitzgerald, Beal, *Career Education and Vocational Guidance*
Frymier, Hawn, *Curriculum Improvement for Better Schools*
Goodlad, Klein, Associates, *Behind the Classroom Door*
Hauenstein, *Curriculum Planning for Behavioral Development*
Higgins, *Mathematics Teaching and Learning*
Hitt, *Education as a Human Enterprise*
Leland, Smith, *Mental Retardation: Perspectives for the Future*
Lutz, *Toward Improved Urban Education*
Meyer, *A Statistical Analysis of Behavior*
National Society for the Study of Education, *Contemporary Educational Issues* (10 book series)
Nerbovig, *Unit Planning: A Model for Curriculum Development*
Overly, Kinghorn, Preston, *The Middle School: Humanizing Education for Youth*
Perry, Wildman, *The Impact of Negotiations in Public Education: The Evidence from the Schools*
Poston, *Implementing Career Education*
Pula, Goff, *Technology in Education: Challenge and Change*
Ressler, *Career Education: The New Frontier*
Rich, *Humanistic Foundations of Education*
Shane, Shane, Gibson, Munger, *Guiding Human Development: The Counselor and the Teacher in the Elementary School*
Swanson, *Evaluation in Education*
Thiagarajan, *The Programing Process: A Practical Guide*
Von Haden, King, *Innovations in Education: Their Pros and Cons*
Weber, *Early Childhood Education: Perspectives on Change*
Wernick, *Career Education in the Elementary School*
Wiles, *Changing Perspectives in Educational Research*
Wiman, *Instructional Materials*

Contributors

James Dator, professor of political science and director of the Program for Futures Research of the University of Hawaii; director of the Research Center for Futures Studies of the State of Hawaii; and advisor to the State Commission on Hawaii 2000

Michael Folk, research associate, Educational Policy Research Center, Syracuse University Research Corporation

Hendrik D. Gideonse, dean, College of Education and Home Economics, University of Cincinnati; formerly director of planning, Bureau of Research, U. S. Office of Education

Arthur Harkins/Richard Woods, director/associate director, Office for Applied Social Science and the Future, University of Minnesota

Willis W. Harmon, director, Educational Policy Research Center, Stanford Research Institute

Norman D. Kurland/William Webster, assistant commissioner, Center for Planning and Innovation/statewide redesign coordinator, New York State Education Department

Michael Marien, research fellow, Educational Policy Research Center, Syracuse University Research Corporation

Edgar L. Morphet/David L. Jesser/Arthur P. Ludka, project director/associate director/assistant director, Improving State Leadership in Education, Denver, Colorado

James M. Oswald, assistant professor of social studies and social science education, Syracuse University; editor, *The Social Science Record;* coordinator, Clearinghouse for Futuristic Studies in the Schools at Syracuse University

Billy Rojas, director, Futuristics Curriculum Project, Alice Lloyd College; former director, Program for the Study of the Future, University of Massachusetts, School of Education

Stuart A. Sandow, research fellow, Educational Policy Research Center, Syracuse University Research Corporation

Harold G. Shane, university professor of education, Indiana University

W. Timothy Weaver, independent consultant, Rye, New Hampshire; associated research fellow, Educational Policy Research Center at Syracuse

Maureen Webster, Cultural Foundations Department, School of Education, Syracuse University; associated research fellow, Educational Policy Research Center at Syracuse

Warren L. Ziegler, co-director, Educational Policy Research Center, Syracuse University Research Corporation; adjunct associate professor of education, Syracuse University

Preface

In an era of uncertainty and change, it is understandable that people are concerned about the future. Even in times of monolithic societal stability, the future was still of concern to all men, everywhere. Traditionally, these concerns about the future were satisfied by mysticism, astrology, sheep entrails, Tarot cards, or I Ching. Given satisfactory "answers," traditional man remained passive about the future, or employed magic to "control" it. In the contemporary era, modern man has enfranchised a new magic, scientific rationalism, to forecast the future—indeed, in the hope once again of controlling it, of mastering the future for human ends.

But more than technical scientific rationalism is now involved. Many people unsophisticated in rational analytic, forecasting, and planning techniques are aware of apocalyptic possibilities, such as nuclear holocaust, eco-catastrophe, the growing strains of overpopulation, and the maldistribution of resources. But is there really a widely-held sense of aggravated urgency to do something about the future? A sense of the future's possibilities—apocalyptic or utopian—has rarely, until the current scene, moved either policy-makers or the man in the street to *intervene* in the present to invent a better future. Indeed, one must seriously question if there is any agreement about what is a better future—for the world, for society, for education.

There is a powerful dialectic of tension between real, human concern about the future and a commitment and capacity to do anything about it. That tension is what this book is really all about. For some people—policy-makers, teachers, students, administrators of educational officialdom—are trying to cleave that tension and go about the business of discovering how to invent, through education, a human future in which mankind not only survives, but survives with hope, dignity, justice, beauty. Still, we are only beginning to learn how to do this, to learn how to translate the "potential of educational futures" into the here-and-now reality of teaching and learning. This volume, a contribution to the growing literature on the future, attempts to provide a rather rapid survey of the increasing number of attempts to relate the futures-perspective to educational planning and policy-making, to pedagogy and curriculum, to the restructuring and revitalization of educative institutions.

Space limitations have restricted this collection to an outline of the *potential* of educational futures. It has many potentials, not all of which are beneficial. The editors hope that we are entering an "age of extending horizons," where our time frame is expanded not only forward into the future but where our scope of appreciation is broadened across disciplines to embrace the full comprehension that is necessary to deal meaningfully with social problems. But paralleling the immense potential of the futures perspective for improved understanding of where we are headed and where we might wish to go—for getting our heads together as the young would say—there are equally great possibilities for faddism, silliness, delusion, and escape. It is to be remembered that a prominent position in the innermost hell of Dante's *Inferno* is designated for those who traffic in false prophecy.

Although this book serves to announce and promote a possible revolution in the way we think and the way we shape our directions, it is also intended, to an even greater degree, to raise many cautions against the *bowdlerization* of a potentially good idea—a phenomenon that should be well known to the astute educator.

The introductory section begins with an outline of a rationale for the futures-perspective followed by an overview of current futurist activity, methods, and ideas. In the second section there are brief, introductory essays on a few of the major forecasting, analytic, and planning tools in the futurist's arsenal. For education in particular, the use of scenarios holds great promise not only as a policy-making tool that can depict a state of affairs at a particular point in the future and/or how this state is arrived at, but also as an educational device that evokes imagination and holistic thinking from students at all ages. The development of new and improved social indicators is also important for education. As the Bureau of the Census slogan tells us, "we can't know where we're going if we don't know where we are."

Futures activity or the lack of it, at the global, national, state, and local school district levels is outlined in the next section. The fourth section includes discussions of the wide variety of futures learning that is available to all age groups throughout the State of Hawaii; an experience in "futurizing" a mammoth and well-known institution, the University of Minnesota; educational futuristics in general, with particular emphasis on college classrooms; and a report on several futures courses and curriculum materials at the high school level. And, in the final section, a distinction is suggested between futurists and futurized specialists and how the "futurization of knowledge" can be furthered.

Again, we emphasize that this book is merely a brief skimming of some of the potential uses of the futures-perspective. At present, they are only potential. Considerable evaluation is required to determine under what conditions the futures approach can make any significant difference in our learning and our lives. What is clear to our authors, and the many educational agencies, institutions, and individuals with whom they work, is that we must learn to use the futures-perspective to make that difference significant.

Michael Marien
Warren L. Ziegler

Contents

Part Three: Applications of the Futures Perspective in Planning

Part Four: Applications of the Futures Perspective in Teaching

Part Five: The Future of Educational Futures

Part One

Educational Futures:
An Introduction
to the Concept

The Potential
of Educational Futures

Warren L. Ziegler

The futures-perspective is an idea whose time has come. Evidence abounds. Some of it is summarized in the following essays which describe the ways in which various educating institutions and systems, at the international, federal, state and local levels, have begun to take a longer-term and more comprehensive look at where they want to go and what they want to do. Further evidence can be found, though not described in this book, in the rapid multiplication of forecasting and longer-term planning activities among private and public research and development, economic, governmental and social institutions. Even in the monastic institution of formal scholarship emerge those academic investigators who have begun to subject that misty and mostly unfathomable territory of the future to the kind of rigorous intellectual inquiry hitherto reserved to the domain of the empirical past. Michael Marien has developed two annotated bibliographies which for the first time assemble and organize this burgeoning array of futures research. (1)

There is still further evidence. An idea has arrived at the point of utilization in the affairs of men when it attracts its critics as well as its supporters. Many of these critics work in those institutions which hold together the fabric of a contemporary world reeling under the hammer blows of change, upheaval, revolution and substantial reform. These institutions make policy in the major sectors of social activity: education and social welfare, production and consumption, relations among nation-states, land and resource utilization, for example. Within these institutions is lodged the formal responsibility for legitimizing that social policy which maintains existing social systems, and which attempts to bring equilibrium and stability to those which, like education, have begun to unravel and uncoil. No prerogative judgment is meant in stating that the function of legitimizing institutions is to conserve the past by utilizing *ad hoc* politics and pragmatic policy to carry it forward into the future.

Some legitimizing institutions perceive this function as the "management" of change in the interest of maintaining "stability." There is a small but growing inclination among governments and education agencies to support serious efforts to look at the present from the viewpoint of the future. The underlying hope is that from the perspective of the future, a rich mixture of expectation and intention, will come guidelines and indicators for policy formation and action in the present.

The most important contemporary example of this conserving responsibility is the formal, core system of schools and colleges. They are specialized institutions for the transference of values, beliefs, skills and knowledge from previous generations to the future by the inculcation of these ideas and competencies, both cognitive and affective, in the youth of society. Indeed, the focus in these essays on the domain of *education* is a profound recognition that among all collective enterprises, education is unique in its claims on the future. The children of this decade will be inhabitants of the 21st Century—*our* future, but *their* present. If, like past generations through the recorded history of mankind, we could still safely assume that the future will be like the present, we could rest easy with the application of past verities to the existential present. But there is a growing suspicion among some teachers, students, administrators and policy makers that the future is going to be sufficiently unlike the past to raise a portentous question about the present aims, contents and structures of education.

The Potential for Education

The issue can now be joined. What is there about the "futures-perspective" whose time has come that might provide assistance in our muddling through, from year to year, in search of solutions to the educational problems of equity, quality, financial crisis, institutional reform, curricular and pedagogical innovation and "relevance." These, and a host of other issues, plague those persons responsible for educational policy making. If there is a potential, what is it?

Potential, of course, means unrealized, unactualized, unconcrete. It is like the future . . . we cannot see, touch, hear, taste, or smell it, and yet it is there, a rich and inevitable product of our imagination. Imagining is a highly suspect activity among "hard-nosed" individuals who pride themselves on their ability and commitment to bring order out of chaos, stability out of change, compromise out of polarity, practice out of theory. Imagination is for the poets, the future is for dreamers, but education—it is widely held—has to do with the humdrum, daily activities of preparing youth to become the carriers into the future of what we adults value, of adult roles, beliefs, behaviors.

Let us understand from the outset that this writer will offer no *proof* that by paying serious attention to the longer-run consequences of the educational present, something better is bound to happen. That proof would have to rest on a knowledge claim about the future. The art of conjecture, as Bertrand de Jouvenel called it, is not yet a science of prediction, particularly in the area of human affairs. (2)

Still, all men, everywhere, not only make claims *about* the future, they actually *claim* the future, they "colonize" it, by every thoughtful and unthoughtful action taken in the present. They do not call themselves poets, dreamers, utopians or inventors. They call themselves pragmatic realists, the most honorific title bestowable upon men of affairs. Note, however, that planning, policy formation, implementation and action are always addressed to the future, never the past. The real issue is only this: is it any longer reasonable to assume that the future will be like the past? Is it any longer reasonable to project an unchanging future from the "lessons" of the past? When we examine the actions of past generations which have reduced, sometimes even destroyed, our options in the present, we are led to a fundamental question: is it desirable and is it possible for human beings to act towards the future in any way substantially different than the ways human beings have always acted towards the future, the unanticipated and unintended consequences of which surround us with the problems and issues of today?

Desirability, in the absence of proof, rests in large measure on the mind-set of individuals who are prepared to address this question seriously. Much of the answer will depend upon a psychological capacity to deal comfortably with ambiguity and uncertainty. Yet that is an individual psychological state which, we must admit, is a scarce item among members of institutions of socialization and social control, whose central function has been to render human life unambiguous and predictable. Indeed, the function of socialization in all societies has been to form the malleable human personality into an instrument which reflects the prevailing modes of behavior, social expectation, conventional wisdom and inherited values. In modern, industrial societies, the specialization of socialization into the formal apparatus of school systems on a massive scale has meant that when these modes and norms begin to break apart—as now appears to be happening—we discover an eruption of disagreement in society about what the schools are for: whom they should teach, what they should teach, when, where and how they should teach, and for what ends.

These questions cannot be answered solely by knowledge. They are also questions of intentionality. The swell of solid research into the behavioral character of learning takes us only so far, and then we are cast upon the rocky shores of that perennial question, "what ought we to do?" Consider, for a moment, what education ought to do about poor and disenfranchised people, who in every modern society are groups of last entry into the formal system of schooling. (3) For them, the schools perform poorly. The schools are not an effective instrument for the induction of these youth into the prevailing modes of moral, political, economic, familial and social behavior. These young citizens do not receive the non-educational benefits bestowed upon that growing majority of our citizens who "make it" through the school system and emerge as full-fledged members of adult society.

Consider what we ought to do in education about the literally scores of millions of adults, both schooled and unschooled, who—increasingly hard evidence suggests (4)—both need and participate in a rich variety of learning activity almost entirely excluded from the dispensing of public funds for the support of education? This may turn out to be the greatest educational scandal of the present era, when we arrive at that future for which adults are unequipped for lack of knowledge, skill and attitude. Some say that future has already arrived.

The argument about the desirability of applying the futures-perspective to education is not resolved, then, by asserting that while a few policymakers, teachers, students, planners, administrators pay a new kind of attention to the future—as described in this collection of essays—most do not. They all do, by reason of the consequences for the future of their present decisions and actions, most of which still rest on the assumption that the future will be much like the present, except perhaps a bit bigger and better. The experience of this generation makes that assumption absurd. But the contrary assumption must lead to more than pious pleading for better times ahead. What stance is it now appropriate for educators to take towards the future?

Three Stances for the Future

From an examination of the literature of educational reform, innovation and planning three different stances towards the future appear to emerge. (5) They are the preventive, the adaptive and the inventive postures which, while never existing in pure form, nevertheless serve as useful heuristic models for examining assumptions about the future which are implicit in all modes of educational action. By far the most prevalent stance is the *preventive,* in which policy is formulated and action taken in the present in such a way as to render a forecast about the future obsolete. Much of educational planning is of this character. A forecast is made which sets forth so disastrous or undesirable a future state of affairs that we intervene in the present to render that forecast false. In this model, the future is considered to be an extrapolation of the past. Under this category would fall crisis planning, with whose consequences we are all too familiar, because attention is paid only to the undesirable forecast. Little or no attempt is made to examine the unanticipated or unintended consequences of intervention, or to relate the forecast to a more comprehensive analysis of other interacting factors, both educational and noneducational.

A second stance towards the future may be called *adaptive*. Here, the forecast is believed to be so powerful, so inevitable, that action in the present is taken to adapt to that emerging state of affairs because, it is held, preventive intervention is neither desirable nor possible. Ten years ago, many educators would have held to the forecast about the inevitability of the whole-scale application of electronic communications technology to problems of teaching and learning. By so doing they set up the agenda of adapting educational structures, curricular contents and pedagogical modes to the assumed power of this technology in order to resolve a host of educational problems most of which had nothing to do with technology but reflected fundamental disagreements over educational aims and standards. Still, the adaptive stance towards the future does engender a more sophisticated and longer-term view.

The third stance may be called *inventive*. Much of the experience described in this collection of essays represents initial efforts to invent a future which, in some substantial ways, is different than our past. This approach is still in its earliest stage of technical formation. It has two key characteristics. The first is the recognition that the future is not a predetermined extrapolation of the past. Rather it is an array of *alternative* futures which can be explicated in some detail and which are comprehensive or holistic views of alternative modes of education as these interact with alternative possibilities in society. The second characteristic is the recognition that the future is the domain of intentional action, of choice, of invention, in which we assume that it is both possible and desirable to engage in acts of creative intervention in the present to bring that desirable future about.

Inventing a Better Future

There is surely no universal agreement about what men would mean by a better future. If it is desirable to commence applying the futures-perspective to all that we mean and do in education, then from the experience of so doing will emerge, in time, a clearer understanding of the standards by which we can judge the desirability of these approaches. Nevertheless, it appears that during the decade of the Seventies we shall see an increasing variety of experimentation and invention in teaching and learning, in institutional formation, in futures casting and analysis, and in policy planning. From this experience we shall acquire a more substantial grounding of what we might come to mean by a more formidable, imaginative and wiser approach to the future of education and society.

From the preceding remarks, it may be observed that the question of the *possibility* of attending to the future in new ways depends a great deal on the courage of those persons who would engage in that enterprise. Whether or not intellectual and administrative courage is in short supply in this country is, of course, a complicated question of definition and fact. We are all teachers and learners in this questive enterprise to invent a better future which relies less on our expectations and more on our intentions. An overweening claim about new approaches to the future is absolutely as counterproductive as the assertion that there is little new in education we can bring about by conscious acts of imaginative intervention and invention. Whatever potential there is in educational futures will be discovered by those for whom discovery and invention is an exciting enterprise, intellectually, emotionally and spiritually. To convey that sense of excitement, and to develop the competencies to engage in that enterprise surely requires an ancient but still marvelous understanding of what education ought to be all about.

Notes

(1) Michael Marien, *Alternative Futures for Learning,* an annotated bibliography (Syracuse: Educational Policy Research Center/Syracuse University Research Corporation, 1971). *Essential Reading for the Future of Education, Revised,* an annotated bibliography (Syracuse: Educational Policy Research Center/Syracuse University Research Corporation, 1971).

(2) For those who want to start at the beginning of modern futures investigation by examing its fundamental epistemology, as distinguished from its application, the "bible" is still probably Bertrand de Jouvenel's *The Art of Conjecture* (New York: Basic Books, 1967).

(3) Charles Nam, *Group Desparities in Educational Participation* (Paris: Organisation for Economic Co-operation and Development, 1971).

(4) See, for example, the work of Stanley Moses, *The Learning Force: A More Comprehensive Framework for Educational Policy,* Occasional Papers, No. 25 (Syracuse: Syracuse University, Publications in Continuing Education, October 1971). And of Allen Tough, *The Adult's Learning Projects: A Fresh Approach to Theory and Practice in Adult Learning* (Toronto, Ontario: Institute for Studies in Education, July 1971).

(5) See, for example, Warren L. Ziegler, "An Approach to the Futures-Perspective in American Education," in *Alternative Educational Futures in the United States and Europe: Methods, Issues and Policy Relevance* (Paris: Organisation for Economic Co-operation and Development, 1971); "Some Notes on How Educational Planning in the United States Looks at the Future," in *Notes on the Future of Education,* Vol. 1, 1, 1969, Vol. 1, 2, 3 (Syracuse: Educational Policy Research Center, 1970).

II

U. S. Futures Research in Education: The Status of the Field in 1972

Harold G. Shane

What Is "Futures Research"?

In an era during which the meanings of words are blunted by misuse and overuse, it seems prudent to begin this statement on "futures research" by defining the term. In its broadest sense, it is concerned with the refinement of the data and the improvement of the processes through which policy decisions are made. The futures researcher or team is concerned with helping policy makers choose wisely among alternative policies and courses that are open to leadership in any given field: government, business and industry, the military, education, and so on.

Futures research with a bearing on education does not merely concentrate on providing advice to those engaged in policy making. It is also intended to help the policy maker himself become capable of recognizing alternative futures, their probable consequences and the "best" courses for one to follow—hopefully in the interest of the general welfare. Persons in futures research often may be seen, therefore, as basically concerned as much with the tutelege of the policy maker as with advice *per se*.

How does futures research differ from conventional planning of future policies? Since man has for centuries engaged in some sort of planning in an attempt to control the course of events, what is new or unique about futures planning as distinct from conventional planning? Current work being carried on by specialists in policy research and futures planning suggests a number of sharp distinctions. Here are five distinctions made by such specialists during interviews conducted by the writer during 1971-1972:

1) Futures planning stresses future alternatives rather than linear projections; it is inherently value directed and action oriented. It concentrates on identifying consistencies and relationships among future probabilities and their probable impact as a result of policy decisions.
2) Futures planning opens up more possibilities than conventional linear planning; it endeavors to point up possibilities that often are overlooked.
3) Conventional planning tends to be based on the assumption that a "good" tomorrow is simply a utopian version of the present with its problems removed. Futures research recognizes that we may need to anticipate quite different tomorrows with respect to resources, values, practices, and the attitudes which they reflect.
4) Futures research depends more on the rational study of anticipated developments—often long range developments and their consequences—than on statistical analyses and projections. Conventional planning is often based on mathematical models. Futures research is less "mathematics model-based" and more "personal simulation-based."
5) In futures planning the emphasis is not on the reform of the past but on creating a probabilistic environment of alternative possibilities and consequences for careful study and choice. (1)

While other nuances of meaning can be added, the five above are a good speculum of current opinion.

Who Is Engaged in Futures Research?

The range and variety of persons, groups, and institutions interested in the improvement of policy decisions through futures research virtually defy description in a short essay. Indeed, it would be a problem to categorize them in any fashion, since they appear to lend themselves only to individual description. In the broadest terms, the "Joseph's Coat" of education-related policy research includes in its many-colored folds such entities as the following:

1) Large corporate entities, notably Rand Corporation (Santa Monica, California), which may be characterized as the "mother of U. S. Futurists," (2) and large industrial complexes such as The Singer Corporation.
2) Non-profit organizations, such as the Rand Spin-off Institute for the Future (Middletown, Connecticut and Menlo Park, California), which engage in comprehensive studies and consultation services for education, government, and industry.
3) The Futures Group of Glastonbury, Connecticut, a profit-making consulting organization and Institute for the Future

Spin-off, which provides computer-based subscription services on expected changes in social indicators, as well as surveys, lectures and workshops, and consultation services.

4) Educational Policy Research Centers, funded by the USOE and located in the Stanford Research Institute and the Syracuse University Research Corporation, designed to assist educational policy makers to develop a capacity for decisions based on an increased insight into alternative futures. (See essay by Gideonse in this volume)

5) Public and private commissions, such as the Carnegie Commission on Higher Education, which find it necessary to consider the future—although generally in a narrow sense.

6) Predominantly individual scholars such as John R. Platt of the Mental Health Research Institute and Donald N. Michael of the Institute for Social Research, both at the University of Michigan, Ann Arbor. (3)

7) Modest ventures in higher education such as the "Program for the Study of the Future in Education," operated on a shoestring and fueled by the enthusiasm of a dozen or two doctoral students at the University of Massachusetts. The former director of this program, Billy Rojas, is now leading another modest venture, "The Futuristics Curriculum Project" at Alice Lloyd College, Pippa Passes, Kentucky.

8) Rare state-funded centers such as The Office for Applied Social Science and the Future, University of Minnesota, which has a central U. S. focus specifically concerned with (a) developing graduate and undergraduate courses and degree programs on alternative futures, (b) campus research and development, and (c) the campus-community interface in the future including work "with large corporations reevaluating their roles in American society." (See essay by Harkins and Woods in this volume.)

9) Author-editor futurists such as Edward Cornish who is President and editor of *The Futurist,* published bimonthly by the World Future Society, which has a Washington, D. C. office. In the same small group is Guy F. Streatfeild who edits the British Journal *Futures* from an office in Guildford just outside London.

10) Conventional educational survey groups such as the Academy for Educational Development in New York City, of which Alvin Eurich is the head, and which recently produced *National Planning for Education* under a USOE contract.

11) Various persons holding USOE grants and contracts which are methodically and deliberately futures-oriented and involve professional futurists. An excellent case in point: The Study Commission on Undergraduate Education and the Education of Teachers directed by Paul Olson at the University of Nebraska, Lincoln.

Some Tools in Futures Research

Although some readers are probably familiar with some of the basic tools used by futurists, in the interests of comprehensiveness some of the well-known ones (the computer, for example) are included along with the more exotic, such as cross-impact analysis.

Perhaps the most important "tool" of the futures researcher is one of the oldest known to man: *human reasoning power.* But where conventional reasoning often tends to be based on the known and the examined, the futurist's reasoning often is "lateral." He is concerned with innovations, speculation, with probing "system breaks" and "counter intuitive" conclusions and concepts. (4) In fine, he endeavors to contemplate the unthinkable and foresee the unforeseen to an extent rarely attempted in human, biological, technological, and sociological contexts, except by such prescient writers as H. G. Wells and Aldous Huxley.

One of the long-familiar tools of the futurist is the *computer.* Here again, however, futures or policies research sometimes departs from conventional practice. One group, for instance, has developed a storage and retrieval system for the producing and analyzing of forecasted events. These are concerned with potential technological changes; prospective social changes (political, demographic, economic); likely management changes with a bearing on business, labor, government, education, and so on. Michael Folk's essay in this volume supplies important caveats for education-relevant application.

The *Delphi technique,* pioneered in the 1950's by Olaf Helmer and Norman C. Dalkey, is perhaps the most widely used tool developed for purposes of future policies research. Based on the premise that many heads are better than one—or as Carl Sandburg phrased it, "Everybody is smarter than anybody"—Delphi is a procedure for refining group judgment through reasoned conjectures on subjects open to speculation. An example: how long may it be before a virtually foolproof contraceptive will be developed for use as an additive in flour or beer. Participants chosen for the highest qualifications go through several "Delphi steps" including the refinement of prospective developments in a given field, the time and probability of their occurrence, estimates of possible consequences, their desirability or undesirability, policy alternatives that are open for mediating consequences, and documentation of opinions relating to each step. For important caveats with respect to the use of Delphi Technique in education, see W. Timothy Weaver's essay in this volume.

Trend extrapolation is another tool of the futurist, one that has been refined as well as borrowed. While based on the assumption that historical time series data are likely to be projectable, futures researchers are likely to emphasize the caveats and alternatives that must supplement extrapolations.

Means of approximating the "behavior" or operation of complex systems are yet another device of value in futures planning. Known as the *simulation model,* this tool comes in at least three varieties: 1) the computer assisted game which involves patterns of interaction among players, and 2) mathematical models in which equations perform the function of describing a given system. Also, 3) there is the actual pencil-and-paper and the three-dimensional model which can be utilized in a number of forms: to depict proposed construction in an urban area, to show complex chemical relationships, to portray interrelationships among varied possible futures, and so on. Jay Forrester, for instance, has developed highly involved computer-generated simulation models for the 250-year life cycle study of urban areas, while members of the Educational Policy Research Center of the Stanford Research Institute, have created forty feasible future histories extending to 2050 A.D. with unique two dimensional and three dimensional simulation models.

Scenarios, like the Delphi technique, are a well established device for designing the future. Herman Kahn and Anthony Wiener in *The Year 2000* speak of scenarios as "hypothetical sequences of events constructed for the purpose of focusing attention on causal processes and decision points." (5) They go on to say that the scenario is intended to answer two types of questions:

1) Precisely how might some hypothetical situation come about, step by step?
2) What alternatives exist, for each actor, at each step, for preventing, diverting or facilitating the process?

In order to isolate parameters that can be correlated, *factor analysis* and *multiple correlation analysis* frequently can be employed in policies research. Somewhat related, and based on quadratic equations, is *cross-impact analysis.* This is a technique for the systematic exploration (in terms of probabilities) of the mutual interactions among forecasted events (that is, how each may mediate the others and, in turn, be mediated), and the spectrum of possible policy decisions to which the cross-impaction points. A corollary of cross-impact analysis is trend impact analysis which involves correlation and assessment of the interaction of possible future events that lend themselves to forecasting.

Experience compression techniques round out this foray into the list of tools (and the jungle of terminology!) that is becoming associated with futures studies. "Experience compression," as the name clearly implies, is based upon the development of intensive futures planning workshops. Here key personnel in a field such as education work together in a structured conference procedure for, say, one to two weeks. During this interval the participants are confronted with probabilistic developments and possible alternative futures in their specialty or field of expertise; developments which require policy decisions which might occur during an academic or calendar year. The quality of choices among identified alternatives open to the individual are assessed during the closing days of the compressed experience.

Some Questions and Ideas from Futures Research

The pay off in futures research will reside in the answers to at least three long-term questions:

1) Have forecasts, scenarios, and so on provided a reasonably accurate picture of possible terrains of the future?
2) Have policy decisions based on futures research proved of service to the general welfare?
3) Has the creative thinking of futurists been so seminal as to have influenced policy decisions in desirable ways and help to insure wise choices among possible alternative futures?

While it is much too early to answer any of these questions with certainty or even confidence—the data simply are not in—it is possible to conclude this essay with a brief description of a few ideas which the writer found stimulating while interviewing some sixty specialists in futures research during 1971-1972. These ideas, in no particular order of significance, reflect the writer's personal biases and perhaps his naivete in selecting them. Granted. But for what they are worth, here they are.

1) Mankind has developed a real potential, however ineptly exercised, for manipulating the environment and for influencing the genetic inheritance of his posterity.
2) Severe ecocrises may confront us, but opinions vary (from 5-10 years to 60-80 years) as to the grace time that remains.
3) There is a need to concentrate on short term (10-20 year) futures planning because of urgent ecological problems and because long-range (50-100 year) speculations are often not action-related and can even be a kind of opiate keeping us from action.
4) We face a number of major crises: the value crisis, a "crisis of transformation" (because half of the developments of the past 50,000 years have occurred in the past 50), and an identity-authority-credibility crisis.
5) One of our pressing social questions is—"What constitutes equity?" both within our society and in a have/have-not world in which the U. S. with 6% of the population consumes about 65% of the world's GNP.
6) The impact of rapid changes which have shaken us since *circa* 1940 should begin to top off. Since we are capable of overkill, have speed-of-light satellite communication (both audio and visual), can transport men to the moon and photo satellites to

Mars, have reduced travel to a two hour trans-atlantic supersonic junket, and have increased data processing about 10^6 or about one-millionfold in forty years, the impact of such socially upsetting changes should diminish as we become used to living with them. On the other hand, the most difficult adjustments to "future shock" may lie in the future.

7) Out of many possible futures that lie ahead on the course the U. S. is now following, most are undesirable; major changes in the trends in our worldwide ways of life are badly needed.

8) Despite some theorists who demonize technology, a wiser and better controlled use of more technology is needed to extricate us from many of our contemporary problems.

9) In the U. S. we may well be on the threshold of a form of "neo-Victorian" conservatism (minus certain conspicuous abuses of humans from the past century) as new values are explored in the later 1970's.

10) While changes of a major nature are required, for example in education, they probably can and should be made within the framework of the established social order in the U. S. At the same time, the needed changes greatly transcend mere reform: present-day America is likely to be sundered in an evolutionary and wholesome manner even as a chrysalis is torn by the wholesome life that emerges from it.

11) Ideas of work, family life, and the role of government will need to be modified appreciably before there is a "topping off" of human problems comparable to the coming "topping off" of the impact of the exponential rate of change.

12) Great confidence must be placed in the power and importance of improved education as a means to improve the lot of mankind on a world basis, but profound changes are required in our interpretation of "education," its goals, and current interpretations of teaching and learning, as reflected in the extensive writing dealing with alternative schools and alternatives to schools.

13) A lifelong educational continuum of great flexibility and variety is needed to replace the current structure of education in the U. S. This should extend from age two or three to old age, compulsory education should be relaxed, and serious heed should be given to the postponement of university study beyond the community or junior college level.

14) In efforts to improve society we sometimes tend to look at the wrong indicators or to make the wrong inferences from our data. (e.g., inferring population projections on trends, rather than including a consideration of changing values and new birth control technologies.)

15) Power and material shortages and greater ecological responsibility probably will eventuate, by the 1980's, in a concept

of "dynamic contraction" rather than the "unlimited expansion" of business and industry. A 1930-type depression could presage such developments of a "steady-state society."

16) We have not yet developed a "coping doctrine" in U. S. democracy that enables us to deal with the phenomenon that most people apparently seek socioeconomic equality with the top ten percent of the population and are, therefore, anti-egalitarian without realizing it.

17) It is important for us to learn how to reconcile *mass* participation in choosing among alternative futures with the expertise of futures research specialists and government-industry-military leaders with privileged information who inherently constitute an elite and a potential meritocracy.

Points such as the seventeen above, by their breadth, depth, and cross-import clearly suggest the need for more extensive policy research and futures planning. They also imply a great need both for vigilance and for enlightened self-interest policies on the part of mankind in sketching the outlines of a world civilization—a temporal "city of man" to replace the "Celestial City" of 1300—or perhaps to pave the way to it!

Notes

(1) The five statements are based on comments made by Theodore Gordon, Thomas Green, Willis Harman, Warren Ziegler, and Olaf Helmer during a 1971-72 survey of the status of future research for the U. S. Office of Education.

(2) A major offspring of Rand is System Development Corporation which Paul Dickson in *Think Tanks* (New York: Atheneum, 1971) describes as "a catalyst in adapting of the spaghetti-like ganglia of the digital computer to virtually everything . . ." (p. 119).

(3) The list of *individuals* who have contributed to futures studies could be extended greatly. Prominent among them would be Gerald Feinberg, Daniel Bell, John McHale, and Jay W. Forrester, to name a few.

(4) A "system break" is an unexpected, major development which changes a society: e.g., the Black Plague of the Middle Ages, a major war or revolution, development of an unprecedented technology. "Counterintuitive" refers to findings leading to conclusions contrary to commonly held assumptions: e.g., 20th century conclusions contrary to 19th century assumptions regarding speeds at which man can travel.

(5) Herman Kahn and Anthony J. Wiener, *The Year 2000: A Framework for Speculation on the Next Thirty-Three Years.* (New York: Macmillan, 1967).

Part Two

Modes
of Viewing
the Future

III

Long-Range
Societal Futures

Willis W. Harman

What are the aims of future-oriented policy research? What sorts of tools are available to carry out the job? What kinds of useful outputs can be anticipated? These are the sorts of questions we wish to address here.

Aims of Future-Oriented Policy Research

Every one in a position of making or influencing educational policy would like to think he is making policies which are:

1) Designed in the context of (a) understanding of second- and higher-order consequences, (b) a long-term strategic perspective, and (c) coordinated actions among diverse agencies and institutions

2) Implementable through actions which can reasonably be expected to accomplish intended objectives

3) Perceived as legitimate by the various stakeholder groups involved

In fact, he typically has neither the time nor the resources to realize his ambition. The federal or state official is likely to be besieged by short-term mandates, subjected to the demands of immediate emergencies, and constrained to pay attention to current operations.

What, in addition to the resources ordinarily available to him, would the policy maker need to bring these extra dimensions to his policy deliberations? Useful policy analysis falls at three levels of relevance:

1) *Comparison of policy alternatives* in the area of the policy maker's responsibility, with particular attention to how they relate to major societal problems and broad societal trends.

2) *Exploration of possible broader state or federal actions* which extend beyond the area of the policy maker's direct responsibility but would involve coordinated action of his agency with others.

3) *Exploration of possible societal changes* which might allow resolutions of problems not otherwise satisfactorily resolvable (of interest both because they are worth monitoring, and because they are relevant to the leadership role of highly placed officials).

J. R. Platt (1) has emphasized the usefulness of a map of "alternative paths to the future," both as a context for anticipating the congeniality of a particular policy in various alternative futures, and as a means of establishing legitimacy through conflict resolution or reduction (e.g., to help contending stakeholders distinguish disagreements over what path to follow). In terms of the three levels of relevance above, a map of alternative "future histories" provides a context within which alternative policies can be examined for suitability in different futures. (One policy might look good in all likely futures; another might be superb if society goes one way, and very ill advised if it goes another.) Furthermore, insofar as major policy thrusts have significant effect on the future direction of society, the second- and higher-order effects of these policies want to be examined in the context of overall systemic change.

In general, systematic policy analysis tends to comprise more or less the following steps: establishment of some sort of model of the system to which the policy is to apply and some description of its societal context; identification of implied assumptions in present policies; delineation of the respects in which the present state of the system differs from some desired state; generation of a set of alternative policies; comparison of these alternatives on the basis of various appropriate criteria, including their probable consequences in each of one or more alternative futures of the broader society; identification of new aspects of the situation which have appeared along the way, and of significant uncertainties; and further clarification of key relationships and iteration of the whole sequence. The gains to be obtained from doing this against a back drop of long-range alternative "future histories" are (a) *generation of new alternatives* which might not otherwise have come to mind, and (b) *addition of new bases for comparison* of policy alternatives, specifically the degree to which they "fit" in, or tend to move the society toward, various alternative futures.

Let us look briefly at some ways of building this background and at some examples of conclusions emerging from such analysis.

Available Tools

Only one systematic approach to generating alternative "future histories" will be mentioned here. Because of its morphological emphasis this approach is particularly suited to social policy research. (2) The state of society is represented by a code word, each digit of which refers to the assumed state of a particular sector of the society (e.g., E_3—economic depression, free enterprise, low government control; E_4—economy prosperous, expanding, with strong government control; S_5—active science and technology with strong environmental focus). Each permutation of digits represents a different state of the overall society—for example, if we consider 10 sectors (digits) and half a dozen possible states for each, the total number of possible states (possible code words) is over fifty million. But most of these are extremely improbable. If, for instance, the combination E_3S_5 is determined to be unlikely, then all states in which that pair occurs are eliminated. (The power of the method lies partly in the fact that the questions to be asked are broken down to molecular and hence tractable form—such as whether E_3S_5 can occur, or whether one specified state can follow directly after another.) After it is determined which states are feasible, the next determination is which sequences of states, say for the next thirty years, are plausible. Iteration is used to obtain self-consistency within the whole pattern. The aim is to obtain the range within which feasible "future histories" may lie—in other words, to get an idea of the range of contingencies which must be planned for.

Figures 1 and 2 show some example results from this method. They are not meant to portray quantitative information except in the roughest sense. Because the most important characteristics of the society from the standpoint of education—e.g., values, fundamental beliefs, attitudes, perceived needs—are not conveniently quantifiable, to introduce quantitative information in the process of roughing out the "future histories" would be to introduce an unknown bias. Once the skeletal outlines of the "future histories" are obtained, all relevant quantitative data can be added.

As stated earlier, the uses of such a "tree" of alternative "future histories" are twofold. Any policy under consideration is going to have to "live" in one of these futures; thus it is useful to test it in several diverse futures. Secondly, the divergencies between the paths comprise one kind of description of major societal policy issues. Overall policy thrusts can be thought of as attempts to move off one path and onto another, and the "tree" forms a useful context for examining the interrelationships between specific policies in various areas and overall systemic change.

Clearly the kinds of results displayed in Figures 1 and 2 are skeletal only. A great deal of "flesh" needs to be added to the skeletons before the descriptions are rich enough to form an adequate backdrop for policy making. One way of doing this is to compose "scenarios" for the paths to make them "feel" more like the real world. Another is to make use of historical comparison; this is particularly valuable at the present point in time, since it is probable that we are living through a period of rapid and revolutionary change which has some characteristics in common with other revolutionary periods. (3)

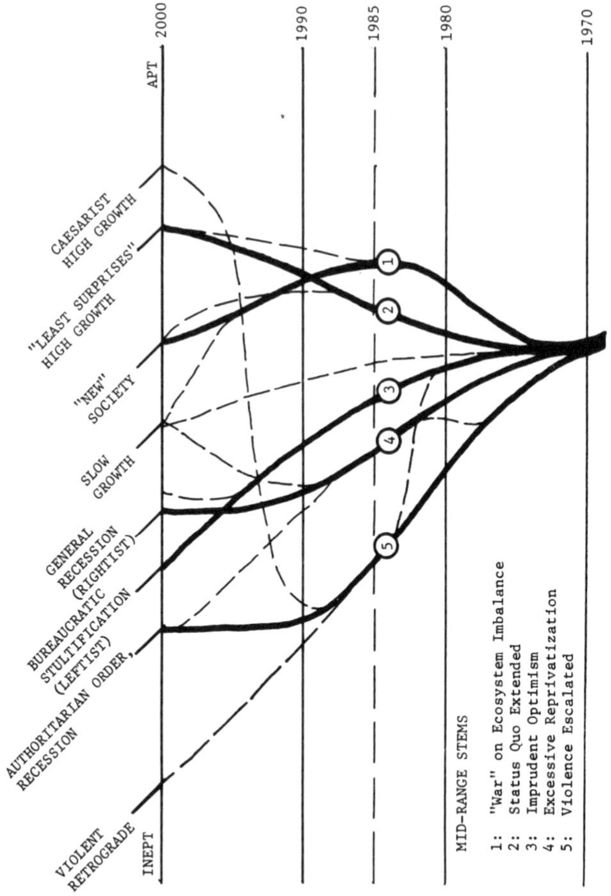
2000
1990
1985
1980
1970
APT
INEPT
CAESARIST HIGH GROWTH
"LEAST SURPRISES" HIGH GROWTH
"NEW" SOCIETY
SLOW GROWTH
GENERAL RECESSION (RIGHTIST)
BUREAUCRATIC STULTIFICATION (LEFTIST)
AUTHORITARIAN ORDER, RECESSION
VIOLENT RETROGRADE
MID-RANGE STEMS
1: "War" on Ecosystem Imbalance
2: Status Quo Extended
3: Imprudent Optimism
4: Excessive Reprivatization
5: Violence Escalated

FIG. 1

"Tree" of alternative future histories (apt-inept dimension)

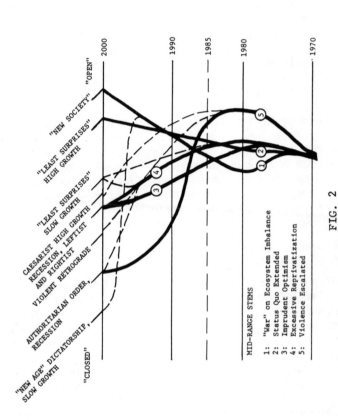

FIG. 2

"Tree" of alternative future histories (open-closed dimension)

Various other approaches can be used to contribute to a more adequate interpretation of the present state of society and the major branchings (key choices) in the near-term future. Condorcet, in 1793, by paying attention to changes in certain fundamental cultural characteristics, was able to make some remarkably accurate forecasts of events to come. (4) Table 1 summarizes a similar attempt for the U. S. in the present time.

Another fruitful approach proved to be a listing of manifest societal problems and a deliberate expansion of the context of these to see the meta-problems to which they lead. Still another amounted to heeding the dictum of the anthropologist Levi-Strauss that "the conventional view of social reality always contains falsifications of the actual state of affairs, and the social institutions function to perpetuate that view." When attempted policies fail conspicuously, as in the attempt to use the schools to reduce socio-economic class distinctions, one might search for ways in which the conventional view of social reality may be hiding important aspects of the actual state of affairs.

It is true that this compressed listing of approaches to an interpretation of available futures has less the characteristics of a systematic methodology than of a recipe for a fruitcake. But the search for truth is seldom systematic, however comforting it may be to believe it can be. Let us now turn to an example of the kind of conclusions we can expect to draw from such a mélange.

A Basic Systemic Problem: Unsatisfactory Macrodecisions

The sorts of analysis discussed above appear to lead to a conclusion which is so far reaching that it affects most major aspects of educational policy. It is the following. Industrial societies in general, and this nation in particular, are faced with one fundamental problem which is so pervasive and so pernicious that the related societal problems (e.g., poverty, unemployment, inflation, environmental deterioration, crime, alienation) will defeat all attempts at solution until it is satisfactorily resolved. *Such resolution hinges on substantial value change in the society.*

This problem is not a new one, and it has long been discussed in the field of economics. However industrial and technological advances have given it new exigency. It is the problem that the *microdecisions* of individuals, corporations, and other groups and institutions (e.g., to buy a certain product, to employ a man for a particular task, to apply a new technological advance) *are not combining to yield satisfactory macrodecisions* for the overall society (e.g., to preserve the physical environment, to provide citizens with suitably rewarding work opportunities, to foster high quality of life). (5)

Some specifics will illustrate:

1) *The "tragedy of the commons."* Microdecisions regarding

TABLE 1

Bases for Forecasting Broad Social Trends

	Condorcet example (1793) (Daniel Bell analysis)	USA 1971 (EPRC/SRI analysis)
Forerunner values	Equality	The individual--self awareness, expression, Person-centered society Ecological awareness Declining significance of property
Processes of diffusion	Printing	Mass media (visual mode)
Forerunner modes of thought	Scientific method	"Alternative futures" "Supraconscious choice" (supplementing the Freudian concept of subconscious choice)
Environmental changes	(Beginnings of Industrial Revolution)	Cybernation; unneeded people Human determination of environment, "Faustian powers" of technology
Changing perceptions	Scientific order	Teleological universe, transcendental order (not, as previously, conflicting with scientific materialism, but complementing it)
Predictions	Political reform and revolution . Social insurance for aged and needy Education public and universal Inequality between persons reduced Women gain equal rights	Synthesis of work-play-growth Reconstructed economic institutions reflecting new values; "humanistic capitalism" Guaranteed income and working/learning opportunity Lifelong education; "Learning Society" Expanded ownership of wealth-producing organizations Coordinated participative planning network (local to planetary)

utilization of resources (e.g., land, air, water, fuels, minerals), which are reasonable from the viewpoints of corporate management and stockholders, developers, and local governments, result in macrodecisions of resource depletion, environmental degradation, urban crowding, which are unsatisfactory to society at large.

2) *Insufficient work opportunity.* People need opportunities to contribute meaningfully to the society and be affirmed in return (commonly with wages). Individual decisions to create and accept jobs fail to result in a satisfactory full employment policy, and thus lead to the incongruity that work opportunity becomes considered as a scarce commodity that needs to be rationed.

3) *Unintended technological impact.* Even with "technology assessment" we don't know how to preserve market microdecision-making regarding technological innovation and yet achieve satisfactory macrochoices with regard to technological disemployment, quality of the environment, infringements of human rights, interference with natural recycling processes, and resource depletion.

4) *Inflation.* Decisions to pass productivity increases from technological innovation on to workers in the form of increased wages, rather than apply them to reducing prices to consumers (plus demands for similar increases for service-sector workers whose productivity is not appreciably increasing), have contributed to persistent inflation.

5) *Alienation.* There is presently a widespread perception that individual, corporate, and government decisions have been guided by such principles as economic growth as a self-justifying end, "the business of business is business," the affluent society, the underdeveloped world as supplier of raw materials for that affluent society, and the "technological imperative" that any technology that *can* be developed and applied *should* be—and that this fact is leading the world toward an intolerable future. Further, individuals feel themselves forced by pressures of "the system" to act in ways that they perceive as neither what they want to do, nor what would be in the general social good. The result is a serious alienation from the society and its institutions.

It is not necessary to examine in detail how it was that the free enterprise system worked as well as it did in the past. What is new is what has been termed the "faustian powers" of modern technology and industry. (6) The physical, technological, social, and psychological environment; the physical and psychological processes of human beings; human nature and the genetic transmission of the human race—all are significantly and to an increasing extent modified by human choice. There is no justification for assuming that choices made on the basis of economic factors will add up to social policy whose long-term effects will be congruent with the highest human goals—or for that matter, will ever produce a tolerable society.

The failure to do so is particularly pronounced in the matter of linking individuals into the larger society. People need opportunities to contribute meaningfully to the society and to gain affirmation in return. The responsibility of the society to provide these opportunities is recognized in this nation's full employment policy. However, the whole thrust of industrialization and technological advance has been to replace men by machines, or to diminish men by the knowledge that they could be replaced by machines.

One approach to the resolution is the continuation of the collectivist trend which has characterized the past four decades. As the unsatisfactory outcomes of self-interest microdecisions adding up to intolerable macrodecisions become manifest, those portions of the system are turned over to the government to regulate and manage. Undesirable as it may be to have individual decisions increasingly regulated by government through coercive controls and manipulative incentives, the alternative of aimless blundering into the future seems even less desirable.

There is another approach, namely that of educating people to make microdecisions which will, with a minimum of imposed regulation, sum to acceptable macrodecisions. This involves both a change in the operative values of the society's institutions and changes in those institutions themselves. There are what may be precursors of this approach in the various pressures toward increased social responsibility of corporations being brought to bear by consumer and citizen groups. But these moves are only a beginning. Nothing short of a distinctly new form of a free-enterprise system can provide the synthesis reconciling the present discrepancy between good business policy and good social policy, on the one hand, and the centrally planned state on the other. In this new capitalism corporate goals would broaden to include, besides the present economic and institutional goals, authentic social responsibility and the personal fulfillment of those who participate in the corporate activity—not as a gesture to improve corporate image nor as a moralistically undertaken responsibility, but as operative goals on a par with profit-making and institutional security. Not production, but productiveness in human life, would be the goal. Barring some catastrophic collapse of the present economic system, large corporations will play a dominant role in the future of this nation and the world. The quality of that future depends, then, on the operative goals of those corporations.

But this "post-industrial" society, whatever its more detailed characteristics, must answer the question of how men shall occupy the portion of their time that is not required to provide goods and services and keep the essential processes of the society functioning. Learning is the major such activity that is nonpolluting, nonstultifying, humane, and socially beneficial. Thus one approaches Robert Hutchins' "Learning Society," (7) which has transformed "its values in such a way that learning, fulfillment, becoming human, had become its aims *and all its institutions were directed to this end.*" Frequent rhetoric about "continuing education" has seldom been taken this seriously—yet this is where the question "What is a society for?" inexorably leads.

Realistic Policy Making

Here have been sketched briefly some characteristics of one alternative future, in which a fundamental problem of the society, and a fundamental political, social, moral, and spiritual crisis approach resolution. Other less desirable "future histories" are easy enough to delineate. The question to face, in concluding, is how this sort of analysis can be useful to on-the-firing-line policy makers.

Think of three kinds of forces producing change in the system: 1) programs for deliberate change, 2) outside events directly forcing change, and 3) societal changes which both force some changes and free up the system to allow other deliberate changes which would not otherwise have been possible.

Familiar examples of the first abound. Programs are instituted to improve education of the disadvantaged, to provide a new focus of "career education," to raise quality of performance by emphasizing accountability for defined outcomes, to alter process through research and innovation. Almost invariably the results are less than were hoped for. Over and over again is demonstrated the truth of the proposition that *educational problems are largely a consequence of, and require change in, factors outside education.* The educational system displays a remarkable ability to change appearances, and to absorb new programs without undergoing fundamental alteration. Thus the educational reform brought about by attempts at deliberate change is limited.

Two examples of the second, outside-the-system change-producing force will suffice. The growing influence of collective bargaining is bringing other changes besides increased teacher salaries. Decisions relating to special duties, frequency and duration of staff meetings, and numerous other aspects of teacher-school relations, once perhaps made by the principal, now become set by negotiated contract. The net result is that in some respects at least the principal becomes more of a routine administrator and less of an educational leader. Other changes, perhaps in the end far more transforming, are coming about through changing patterns of school finance resulting from a combination of political pressures for property-tax relief and court decisions relating to between-district inequities in funding.

The third kind of force for change, societal trends, is illustrated by the preceding discussion of a fundamental systemic problem, the failure of individual microdecisions to add to tolerable macrodecisions. One can attribute the failure of the society to make real progress with the problem of the disadvantaged (including the failure of the schools to reduce barriers between socio-economic classes) to the intractability of this underlying problem, as well as the failure of vocational education courses to make black ghetto youth employable, and numerous other failures imputed to the schools.

Now relate these three types of forces for change to three kinds of action available to policy setting agencies. First, they can institute and carry out various kinds of programs designed to effect deliberate change. Proposed policies should certainly be examined in the context of more than one alternative future, since some will be congenial to one "future history" but quite inappropriate if history takes a different course. The probable effects of anticipated outside forces need to be brought in if the programs are to be appropriate to a changing situation. Furthermore, in view of the limited effectiveness of such programs it is important to communicate realistic expectations of outcomes. Overpromising fails to build the kind of public support which will be required if a sustained effort is to be maintained, as would be necessary for any very fundamental change.

The fact that the problems of vocational education are not separate from those of unemployment, or that the problems of the disadvantaged child learning to read are not separate from the economic problems of the inner city, suggests that concerted action of a number of agencies and institutions is much more likely to make headway than a like number of separate actions. A "map" of alternative "paths to the future" and an analysis of the fundamental underlying societal problems which must be solved in any "future history" can provide the means by *which diverse agencies can relate their common concerns* and compare the alternatives available to all.

Finally, if the most fundamental problems require value and perceptual changes in the overall society, the policy maker at least knows the limits of programmatic action, even the concerted action of a number of agencies. However, available actions are not yet exhausted. Governments also provide a leadership function. Understanding the full dimensions of an educational problem, including a realistic appraisal of what might be accomplished through deliberate programs and what alternatives are made more or less likely because of extra-systemic events, the policy maker is able in his leadership role to work towards the kinds of value shifts, cultural changes, and elimination of perceptual blocks which could move the society toward resolution of its most fundamental problems.

Conclusion

Much has appeared in the name of "futuristics" or "futurology" which—however entertaining or shocking—is of little direct value to the policy maker. In these brief remarks the writer has attempted to suggest the kinds of exploration of the future, and the kinds of articulation of these with problem-focused analysis, which could be clearly useful in assisting the harried policy maker to make his decisions in the broader context of alternative societal futures.

Notes

(1) Platt, J. R., "How Men Can Shape Their Future," *Futures* (March 1971), pp. 32-47.

(2) Rhyne, R. F., "Projecting Whole-Body Future Patterns—The Field Anomaly Relaxation (Far) Method" (Menlo Park, California: Educational Policy Research Center, EPRC RM-10, February, 1971).

(3) McEachron, Norman B., "Forces for Societal Transformation in the United States 1950-2000" (Menlo Park: EPRC, 6747-RM-13, September, 1971).

(4) Bell, Daniel, "The Art of Forecasting Social Change," *Congressional Record* (January 15, 1969), Vol. 115, No. 9, Senate Proceedings, pp. 3-4.

(5) Harman, W. W., "Key Choices of the Next Two Decades," an address given to the White House Conference on the Industrial World Ahead: A Look at Business in 1990 (February 7-9, 1972).

(6) The term "faustian powers" is discussed in H. Kahn and A. Wiener, *The Year 2000* (New York: MacMillan, 1967).

(7) Hutchins, Robert, *The Learning Society* (New York: Praeger, 1968).

IV

The Delphi
Forecasting Method:
Some Theoretical Considerations

W. Timothy Weaver

The question posed in this essay is, *On what grounds can educators select among forecasting tools?* Several quasi-scientific tools are on the market today comprising, in effect, a policy planners' forecasting kit. Among the most popular of these is Delphi.

What Delphi Is

The Delphi Technique is an intuitive methodology for organizing and sharing "expert" forecasts about the future. Its original use was to establish a chronology of scientific and technological events and to judge when the events might occur through the speculations of several experts. Delphi has been justified primarily on the grounds that it prevents professional status and high position from forcing judgments in certain directions as frequently occurs when panels of experts meet. The intention was to assure that changes in estimates reflected rational judgment, not the influence of certain opinion leaders.

Typically, the procedure includes a questionnaire, mailed to respondents who remain anonymous to one another. Respondents first generate several rather concise statements of events, and in the second round give estimates as to the probability of each event occurring at a given date in the future. Once the respondents have given their answers, the responses are collated and returned to each respondent who then is invited to revise his estimates. The third-round responses are made with the knowledge of how others felt regarding the occurrence of each event. Again, the responses are assembled and reported back to the participants. If a respondent's estimate does not fall within the interquartile range of all conjectures, he is asked to justify his position, whether or not he wishes to change it.

More recently, the technique has been extended to include questions about how familiar the participants are with the events. Respondents are also occasionally asked to rate the desirability of the events, should they occur. In addition, respondents are asked to give some statements about what impacts the events might have, if they occur. Still another question now being asked is what possible "interventions" might be developed to either enhance or reduce the probability that an event would occur.

One of the earliest uses of Delphi in educational planning was O. Helmer's study incorporated as part of the 1965 Kettering project to elicit preference judgments from a panel of education experts and experts in various fields related to education. (1) The purpose was to compile a list of preferred goals for possible federal funding. Just what value this study had is left in doubt by the experimenters. Helmer concludes, "Although we believe that the compilation of a large number of ideas for possible educational innovations has served a useful purpose, not too much weight should be given to substantive findings resulting from these pilot studies."

Two additional Delphis have been conducted and reported as experiments to elicit preference statements from educators or those with a direct interest in education. The studies were considerably more focused than Helmer's experiment. F. R. Cyphert and W. L. Gant used Delphi as an opinion questionnaire to elicit preferences from the faculty of the School of Education at the University of Virginia and other concerned parties. (2) D. P. Anderson used Delphi in a similar way in Ohio but limited the focus to a county school district. (3)

In the Anderson study, statements were obtained from teachers, board members, administrators, and selected educational experts. The statements clustered in two sets: client services and organizational adaptation. Using three Delphi questionnaires, priorities were assigned to each compiled set of goal statements independently, using "zero sum" logic.

In both the Virginia study and the Ohio study, most of the change in priorities occurred after the first modal distribution was reported back to all respondents. Subsequent rounds failed to produce significant changes. The greatest disagreement on particular items in the Virginia study was on preparation of teachers at the graduate level without prior experience and on promoting statewide uniformity of curriculum. The former item, preparation of teachers without experience, was ranked among the top 10 by the groups as a whole, but lowest by organization leaders and politicians. The latter item, a uniform curriculum, was ranked high by the nonteacher organization and low by the university and expert groups.

These education studies differ in principle from the original use of Delphi. In the three studies, respondents were asked to focus on what they would like to see happen, rather than what is likely to happen. However, it is unclear how that difference in focus would change the outcome of either type of experiment. It is not possible at the moment to identify precisely Delphi statements which reflect rational judgment as opposed to feelings of desirability. When the task is speculating on the future, just what assumptions underlie one's responses is unclear—that is, unless those assumptions are specifically and systematically flushed out.

Delphi was also used to develop long-range forecasts stemming from social indicators in a study conducted by the Institute for the Future and sponsored primarily by the Syracuse Educational Policy Research Center. (4) The areas of concern were urbanization, international relations, conflict in society and law enforcement, national political structure, values, and the impact of technology on government and society. The project was part of a larger continuing methodological and substantive study of the future environment in which educational policies enacted in the near future might be expected to have some impact. The study was conceived not to prepare a detailed description of the future, but instead to examine expectations about the future held by persons well informed in several domains of the social sciences. The study was intended to be only an initial step and not a final piece of research.

Delphi has been modified and linked together with other tools, not for the purpose of producing intuitive forecasts, but for the purpose of modifying the awareness, assumptions, and skills of the persons making the forecasts. For example, Stuart A. Sandow constructed a simulation exercise which links together in a logical flow of activities the basic principles of Delphi, cross-impact matrix, scenario writing, and analysis of future histories. (5)

There have been a number of other "first-step" efforts elsewhere to recast forecasting tools such as Delphi into teaching tools. Some of these efforts are unreported to date. The Ghetto 1984 game developed by Jose Villega at Cornell University bears noting as well as the Delphi Exploration game developed at the University of Illinois. (6) It is beyond the scope of this paper to detail these and several other studies not mentioned. (7)

Toward an Effective Critique

In order to critique the Delphi method effectively, one must consider both its process (the way people are asked to handle information about the future), and the plausibility of its product.

Within this context, one may further identify the "family" of forecasting tools with which this article is concerned. It should be understood that Delphi is only one of several "intuitive" exploratory methods. Other methods include future history analysis, scenario writing, and cross-impact matrices.

These tools share some common properties. They employ collective opinion or subjective judgment as basic inputs to the forecasting process in lieu of quantifiable data. In effect, they operate on the principle that several heads are better than one in making subjective conjectures about the future. It is assumed that experts, within a controlled intuitive process, will make conjectures based upon rational judgment and shared information rather than merely guessing, and will separate hope from likelihood in the process. Experts are experts because they are objective, take into account new or discrepant information, and construct logically sound deductions about the future based upon a thorough and disciplined understanding of particular phenomena and how they relate. Simply put, the methods are nondata based and rely on collective expert judgment.

Furthermore, the forecasts do not begin, as do extrapolations, with a demonstration of how future events grow out of specific present or past conditions. That is, these forecasts are not so much projections as they are quantum leaps into some future time frame in which one is left to find his way backward to the present.

It is crucial that these tools heavily emphasize the explanations upon which the plausibility of the forecast rests. An intuitive forecast which carries with it no explanatory quality may be correct, but it would be trivial. That is the singular weakness of Delphi. Delphi forecasts have little substantive explanatory quality in their present form. The plausibility of the Delphic forecast as now construed can be argued only on the basis of expert consensus or agreement. But consensus alone is not a sufficient condition for arguing that a forecast is plausible and convincing. It is not even a necessary condition.

The educational policy implication underlying future studies is that the meaning of any statement about the future will be manifested only in what the statement convinces us the future can be made to be through reasonable actions, not in what it will be. Therein lies a fundamental source of conflict. What the future can be or should be made to be differs drastically in the minds of people. We all carry around a different set of assumptions about the future. The failure to clarify and share such assumptions is a failure of Delphi forecasts. Studying the future is in effect studying assumptions we hold about the future. Stripping bare the underlying assumptions about the future often reveals that (a) we present no alternatives, (b) our thoughts are based upon very naive and weak arguments, and (c) our judgments are the product of linear thinking. As a result, forecasts fail to convince. They offer no reasonable options. It seems fundamental that forecasts will have little value to policy makers unless they open options.

Although the nature of the Delphi method then ought to be such that certain rather important distinctions could be made about forecasts and their underlying assumptions, it is not. For instance, it is not clear how one can discriminate between Delphi forecasts that are the products of "hope" and those that are "probable." It is clear, however, that hope or desirability interferes with and to a considerable extent influences judgments about future events.

A second fundamental distinction needs to be made. In the absence of actually knowing in detail just what the future will be, one can either guess or judge. The very basis of the Delphi forecasting process is opinion as to when an event is likely to occur. It seems important, in establishing the plausibility of such opinion, that it be distinguishable as rational judgment rather than guesswork. Delphi, at present, can render no such distinction, because the arguments which support an opinion are not emphasized unless the opinion is contrary to the group norm.

What we know about how the mind constructs images of the future remains rather puny, but the fundamental assumptions which are generally held about Delphi seem questionable. For instance, the Delphi Technique was created to prevent professional status and high position from forcing judgments in certain directions when panels of experts met. The intention was to assure that through questionnaires, changes in estimates would reflect rational judgment, and therefore not be subject to social psychological factors. Empirical evidence tends to show the naiveté of such an assumption. Three independently conducted studies suggest that within the Delphi procedure individuals who "swing" in from wide ranges to more narrow ranges do so less on the basis of rational argument, examination of evidence, or review of assumptions than because decision-making strategies of certain persons are subject to change as the task is perceived to be less ambiguous, and on account of certain personality factors such as fundamental needs and integrative complexity. (8) These findings, of course, are not unexpected, and generally support the studies of several other investigators. It also seems clear that subjective judgments of even very complex or abstract thinkers may be considerably influenced by their feelings of desirability regarding the future events in question. The assumption that "experts," who may be presumed to be complex thinkers, bring to bear "cool analysis" in their judgments about the future is questionable in light of this finding.

Research questions on forecasting methods must begin to reflect some consideration of the *interaction* between dispositional factors and the conditions in the experiment. Among the more important questions are: How do differences in judgments about the future reflect differences in the self-structures of the people who make the judgments? And consequently, how will differences in estimates be shaped by exogenous variables such as complexity and ambiguity of the task? The failure to consider these questions is a weakness of Delphi studies to date.

Summary

Delphi, like the future it was intended to foretell, has not turned out to be what we expected. There are certain fundamental weaknesses of Delphi in its present form as a forecasting tool. Briefly, they have to do with interpreting the significance of "convergence" of opinion under the conditions imposed by Delphi.

Any consideration of the future of education should attempt to clarify what we can reasonably expect to make happen or not expect to make happen. Rather than a focus on "accuracy," the focus might better be on "plausibility" or reasonableness of forecasts. In that sense Delphi at present comes up short because there is little emphasis on the grounds or arguments which might convince policy makers of the forecasts' reasonableness.

Of equally great importance, however, research also leads to the conclusion that Delphi, in combination with other tools, is a very potent device for teaching people to think about the future of education in much more complex ways than they ordinarily would. When *this* use of Delphi is understood it is found to be a useful instrument for something more important than what it was designed for, namely, a general teaching strategy. What this means is that initially the way to get educators to make better decisions—decisions which account for alternative consequences—is to enhance their capacity to think in complex ways about the future, and Delphi seems ideally suited to such a purpose. Indeed, educators may find in Delphi and other forecasting tools a better pedagogy.

Notes

(1) O. Helmer, "The Use of the Delphi Technique in Problems of Educational Innovations" (Santa Monica, Calif.: Rand Corporation, P-3499, December 1966). 1966).
(2) F. R. Cyphert and W. L. Gant, "The Delphi Technique: A Tool for Collecting Opinions in Teacher Education," paper presented at the AERA symposium on Exploring the Potential of the Delphi Technique by Analyzing Its Application (Minneapolis, Minn., March 4, 1970).
(3) D. P. Anderson, "Clarifying and Setting Objectives on an Intermediate School District's Objectives Utilizing the Delphi Technique," paper presented at the AERA symposium on Exploring the Potential of the Delphi Technique by Analyzing Its Application (Minneapolis, Minn., March 4, 1970).
(4) R. de Brigard and O. Helmer, *Some Potential Societal Developments—1970-1990.* Middletown, Conn.: Institute for the Future, R-7, April, 1970.
(5) S. Sandow, "The Pedagogical Structure of Methods for Thinking About the Future: The Citizen's Function in Planning" (Syracuse, N. Y.: Educational Policy Research Center, Syracuse University Research Corporation, working draft, August 1970).

(6) For an initial description of the Cornell University project see J. L. Pfeffer, "Preliminary Draft Essays and Discussion Papers on a Conceptual Approach to Designing Simulation Gaming Exercises," Technical Memorandum No. 1 (preliminary draft) (Syracuse, N. Y.: Educational Policy Research Center, Syracuse University Research Corporation, October 1968). S. Umpleby, *The Delphi Exploration.* A computer-based system for obtaining subjective judgments on alternative futures, Social Implications of Science and Technology Report F-1 (Urbana, Ill.: University of Illinois, August 1969).

(7) For a review of Delphi's studies, see W. T. Weaver, *Delphi, a Critical Review.* Final Report. (Syracuse: Educational Policy Research Center, December 1971).

(8) Cf. W. T. Weaver, "An Exploration into the Relationship Between Conceptual Level and Forecasting Future Events," unpublished doctoral dissertation (Syracuse: Syracuse University, 1969); R. M. Campbell, "A Methodological Study of the Utilization of Experts," unpublished doctoral dissertation (UCLA, 1966); and J. S. Waldron, "An Investigation into the Relationship Among Conceptual Level, Time Delay of Information Feedback, and Performance in the Delphi Process," unpublished doctoral dissertation (Syracuse: Syracuse University, 1970).

V

Computers and Educational Futures Research

Michael Folk

This paper will attempt to give the reader some understanding of areas of educational futures research in which the computer is particularly useful. It will focus on four areas which are fairly representative of the different possible kinds of computer involvement: 1) a "markov process" model, 2) a "major trend analysis" model, 3) cross-impact matrix analysis, and 4) the focus delphi. The first two are fairly traditional techniques, and each has a substantial history of experimentation and application in many areas. The others are two of many tools recently developed for the specific purpose of probing the future.

For each of the four research techniques we will (a) give a brief description of the tool and its distinguishing characteristics, (b) explore the role of the computer—both psychologically and physically—in the process, and (c) discuss a few of the problems which arise with the tool per se and with the computer's part in the tool, and which we feel ought to be made clear to a planner considering its use.

Traditional Methodologies

Educational systems have characteristics which are measurable. Indeed, some people feel that any characteristic which is truly describable is measurable, and a great deal of data bearing upon these characteristics can be collected. It often seems that the data can be most useful if a theoretical model of the system can be built to describe the various elements of the system and how they are interrelated. If the elements are measurable, it is possible to 1) plug their measures (the data) into the model to find out what the system will look like in the future, or 2) plug various hypothetical data into the model to get an idea of what the system would look like if the conditions represented by the data were to obtain.

Economists have been building models of economic systems for a long time. In economists' terms these models are increasingly more accurate (though they generally do not reflect certain important factors, such as disbenefits to the economy). Therefore educational planners have in large measure drawn from the work of the economists in constructing their models. This has meant that educational models tend to look a great deal like economic models, and, since the models are supposed to give definitions to the systems they model, educational systems sometimes tend to be viewed as economic systems. The first two techniques to be considered owe much of their form to the theory of economic modelling.

Some models include only a few major components; others try to include as many variables as possible, even those that do not seem to have much influence on the total system. Analysis based on models of the first type is called "macro analysis" (like looking at the system from a long way off, so that only the major parts are discernible); "micro analysis" involves trying to take all the little things into account. Both types of analysis can be conceptually complex or conceptually simple; the difference between the two is determined by how finely the system is described in the model.

The first technique to be considered—the markov process—tends to be applied to micro analysis, though a simple macro analysis involving a markov process is not out of the question. The second technique tends to be applied to macro analysis. This distinction between the two techniques partially determines the way in which the computer is used for each.

A Markov Process Model

Some kinds of models attempt to describe the *output* of a system in a certain year in terms of the *state* of the system in that year. A classic example of output is teacher-hours (output) which could be related, simplistically, to the number of primary teachers (p), secondary teachers (s), and the hours taught per teacher (h_p and h_s, respectively), by the formula: (1)

$$\text{Output} = h_p \cdot p + h_s \cdot s.$$

The state of the system in this example would be described by p and s.

Other models might try to tell us how the system changes dynamically over time by relating the *state* of the system in a given year (say, year k+*1) to 1) the state* of the system in the year before (year k), and 2) the *input* to the system (policy decisions made) in that year (k). In a mathematical model such relationships as the two discussed above would be expressed by a set of mathematical equations, and each state and each input would be expressed as a set of numbers; thus, hopefully, these numbers completely describe the system at each year, while the equations completely describe the way in which 1) the state and input at each stage determine the state at the next stage, and/or 2) the state of the system at year k determines the output in that year.

Models of this type are called markov processes because the state of the system in the future is completely dependent on the present state of the system and its inputs and is independent of the way in which the present state developed.

Obviously such models can be used to forecast the state of a system next year (or the output this year), if enough is known about the variables. If planners are able to control the value of certain of the variables, then the model can be used to study the effect on the whole system over a time period of changes in the values of those controllable variables (inputs).

Models of this sort, if they are to be realistic, tend to have a large number of variables and equations, and relationships among the variables tend to be very complicated. The virtue of these models is that they force those who use them to pay careful attention to parts of the system which individually might not have a sizeable influence on the functioning of the system but which for their own sake deserve attention in the context of the larger system. For instance, specific knowledge about the dropout rate from the fourth grade may not be useful in determining production of high school graduates, but seen in the context of the whole K-12 system it may reveal useful information about elementary school organization.

Enter the computer. If it were not for the computer, the researcher would not consider the use of this kind of model as an aid to forecasting. With the computer he can experiment with many different situations over relatively long periods of time. With the computer the model becomes a whole different entity for the researcher. It is not just a way of describing the system, for when the model can so fluently be used to simulate the system, it becomes a dynamic system in itself, it takes on a life of its own, and has a much more powerful meaning for the user. As such, there is always the danger that he will focus on the model as the system with which he is concerned, and the truths of the model will be the truths with which he deals. So the danger in the use of the computer lies not in the possibility that it might do something false, but that what it does it does so well. It is so efficient at executing the simulation, it generates information about the model with such dispatch and certainty, that the user gives it more credibility than it deserves.

There are other dangers, some quite subtle, involved in the use of this medium. For one thing, modellers in their enthusiasm sometimes convince themselves that they have found a measure for a given characteristic when in fact they have changed the characteristic to something other than the one they originally had in mind, in order to produce the measure. In fact all aspects which influence the system may not be measurable; and even if they are measurable, the researcher may not be able to determine directly how they influence the system in any mathematically describable way. Or, if he does determine relationships among the variables, there may be a tendency to substitute more ideologically defined relationships for those that might be determined better by a greater degree of scientific investigation.

Some relationships among the variables may depend heavily on human factors such as individual decisions or responses by influential groups of people to events which themselves might have been quite difficult to forecast, and which may not have been seen as being part of the system under study. The national student strike of 1970 was a response to a political decision which was totally unrelated to education, but which served as a catalyst for discontent that was related to education. The word most used in explanations of fluctuations of the stock market, which is the most modelled system of all, is the word "confidence."

Besides the variables mentioned above, there are other elements of the mathematical formulations which the modeller claims to know. These may be constant, or they may change with time. Their values are usually determined by analyzing past (historical) data, and determining trends which, according to theory, can be used to describe future values. Even if the statistical techniques used for determining these trends are theoretically correct (and one can seldom be certain that they are), the range of the values forecast by these trends is likely to be so broad that a projection of more than two or three years could easily be so far off as to cause the output of the system to be 50% off. Some modellers, recognizing problems such as these, do not pretend to describe systems in terms of their ultimate, atomic components. Instead, they model very small finite subsystems of the total system, accepting that these can only give them some clues to the operation of the larger system, and that the larger system's interaction with *its* environment must also be considered. Thus, it behooves the planner to exercise caution in the determination of these elements and the interpretation of models based on them.

Major Trend Analysis

A technique which on the whole avoids the problems discussed above involves the *aggregation* (by the modeller) of many components of the system in terms of a few reasonably stable general indicators of what the system looks like. This process for forecasting usually involves careful exploration of historical data for stable trends and strong correlations which suggest logical relationships which can be expected to hold in the future.

A typical example of the use of this technique is James C. Byrnes' model (2) for determining the quantity of higher education, which is based on an extensive examination of available data on major long-term trends in higher education, covering areas such as degrees awarded and numbers of students enrolled. Using these long-term series he found certain stable relationships which held with a high degree of certainty over time. He found, for instance, that the ratio of the number of graduates to a relevant population was predictable with reasonable confidence from a frequency distribution based on level of educational attainment over a long period of time.

In effect, Byrnes was able to find certain stable cross-sectional mechanisms that related the long-run institutional data to changes in several aspects of the system over time. From this information about mechanisms and from a few major trends, whose development over time could be forecast with reasonable accuracy, he was able to speculate about implications for education for the next fifteen to twenty years with greater confidence than he would have with a model which tried to include every small detail.

Here the role of the computer was primarily that of a high speed calculator with a great deal of storage: all available figures (such as census data by age for each year from 1900 to 1970, number of degrees awarded by year from 1870 to 1970, etc.) were entered into the computer, then manipulated via the computer to apply statistical techniques in an attempt to determine plausible long-range trends.

Though this kind of model-building is aided by the computer, it does not relegate to the computer the sole responsibility for sorting out complex problems, and hence there is much less danger that the calculations themselves will be viewed as the source of truth. Fortunately, up to now most computer-based modelling has been of this sort, but there is a great deal of good work being done developing elegant and detailed "micro" models of educational systems, work which could be misused if researchers let themselves be seduced by the power of the computer and turn over too much of the responsibility for thinking to the machine.

Futurist Methodologies

The increasing interest across many disciplines in the study of the future has spawned a new trans discipline concerned in part with the development of methodologies specifically designed for studying the future. These methodologies in part owe their existence to the computer, since many would not be operable without the aid of the machine. The two methodologies we will discuss here are the cross-impact matrix technique (CIM) and the focus delphi. CIM relies heavily on the use of the computer; the focus delphi process is aided by, but not dependent on, the computer. Both are methods specifically designed for studying the future.

Cross-Impact Matrix

CIM is a technique for describing and analyzing interactions among a set of possible future events. Actually there are many forms of CIM, but they all work essentially the same way. Input consists of estimates concerning the likelihood of occurrence of the events, data on possible trends, and estimates of the impact that occurrence of each event will have on the probability of occurrence of the others. The output consists of an adjusted probability for each event, calculated on the basis of a formula which uses the trend data, conditional probability data, and the impact.

TABLE 2

A Five-Event Cross Impact Matrix

No.	Events Effect of	Probability	Estimated Year of Occurrence	Impacts Effect on Event No.				
				1	2	3	4	5
1	Laws requiring nego- tiation between school boards and teacher unions	.7	1978	--	10	4	3	1
2	All teachers in unions	.9	1976	8	--	6	8	4
3	Most students in unions	.3	2000	0	2	--	8	9
4	Voucher plan man- datory in half of states	.4	1980	6	8	0	--	10
5	20% in enrollment in "new schools"	.8	1980	-5	-7	6	10	--

For instance, a five event matrix might be displayed as shown in Table 2. The estimated impacts are displayed in matrix form on a scale from -10 to +10, where -10 indicates that the occurrence of the event in the corresponding row would have the strongest possible negative influence on the event in the corresponding column, a +10 indicates the strongest positive influence, a zero indicates no influence, and so forth.

Output (or final probabilities) is achieved by conducting a series of runs and averaging the results, where for each run: 1) an event is chosen at random, and it is "decided" on the basis of its probability whether it has occurred; 2) the probabilities of the remaining events are adjusted according to the formula and whether or not the chosen event occurred; 3) another event is chosen from among the remaining, and the process is repeated until all the events are exhausted. From the data generated in the process, final probabilities for the events are calculated. Many runs need to be made to account for possible differences in the order of occurrence of the events. After a number of runs, all starting with the same input data, reasonably close estimates of the "true" final probabilities can be derived. (3) If the computer is in an interactive mode, then this whole process can be repeated in real time, with adjustments made in that input data which could conceivably be controlled by certain actions, to test the effects of alternative actions.

The first and perhaps for the participant the most valuable part of the CIM exercise involves determining the inputs. This is the stage when the participants are forced to examine very carefully the events which are most important to consider, all the complex interactions among the events, and the likelihood and importance of each event within the whole environment. (4)

The next part of the exercise involves mathematical manipulation of the inputs. For a ten event matrix a minimum of about thirty thousand calculations is required to determine the final probabilities, so the computer is needed for even a single run. As with the markov model, the researcher would not consider the use of this tool were it not for the computer, which gives him the power to experiment with many different possible situations in a short time. Also, as with the model, the computer is so efficient at its task that there is a tendency for the user to focus only on the computer-generated output and not to keep in mind the possible tenuous links between the interactions among events in reality and the interactions that are defined by the formula (and carried out by the computer).

There are other problems. For one thing, CIM deals almost exclusively with subjectively generated forecasting data (as do many of the futurist methodologies), rather than with "hard," verifiable data as did the models. In addition, the markov process model was based on well understood and strictly defined mathematical concepts; the researcher could understand the formulae involved, and indeed, in general it was he who had generated them. The CIM, however, is heavily dependent on mathematics which is manipulative in nature, and often too complicated for the user to understand even if the formulae involved were not highly controversial mathematically. For these reasons the acceptance of the computer generated output is even more dangerous here than with the markov model, for there is much less understanding of what the output really means.

For instance, the initial probabilities are very personal, very biased estimates of liklihood, and can be called probabilities only in the loosest statistical sense. At best they indicate how people perceive the relative likelihoods of each of a set of events, and the reliability of any probability estimate is necessarily affected by the vagueness of our understanding of such concepts as wishful thinking, by the respondents' incomplete knowledge of both the system under study and how the system would respond to different conditions (as opposed to how one thinks it would respond), and by many other "soft" variables. A great deal of research is being conducted at present in an effort to determine how subjective probability fits into statistical theory, and towards identifying the mental models that people have of ill-defined systems.

These and other questionable aspects of methods such as CIM make it foolish to think of them as producing anything but the roughest estimates. (5) They can provide a useful *framework* for thinking about the future, and they can help raise questions that might not otherwise occur to the user, but users should not expect to gain any new information from them.

Focus Delphi

The focus delphi (6) is another area in which the computer has been used in the manipulation of forecasting data. Unlike cross-impact analysis and modelling, the computer is used primarily for efficient storage, retrieval and display of data gathered in the delphi exercise. A small amount of simple statistical work is done, such as determining medians and interquartile ranges among different subsets of the data, but no attempt is made to come up with a strict computable model of anything. The main purpose of the data manipulation is to look at differences between groups' perceptions. While the predictive nature of these differences is of dubious value, they have proved very useful for heuristic purposes.

The focus delphi technique involves obtaining responses from certain groups of people as to when or if each of a large set of related events is deemed likely to occur, what the value of the events is to themselves and to society, and where the source of power lies to enhance or inhibit the likelihood of the events' occurrence. In the computer manipulation of focus delphi data no statistic is forced. For measures of central tendency only median and interquartile range are employed, allowing responses like "later than the maximum time," or "never." The computer generates hard-copy display for each round in such a format that it can be photocopied with a minimum of retouching and sent out as part of the next round questionnaire.

It is not possible to show here the kinds of data generated in a typical focus delphi, but a listing of some of the table headings from one done for the New York State Education Department (7) is indicative:

- Median Date Forecast—Spread (i.e., the difference between the latest median by any group and the earliest median, in ascending order)
- Chronology of Events in Order of Predicted Occurrence
- Changes from Round II to Round III, Averaged Over the Four Groups (including change in median date and interquartile range)
- Changes from Round II to Round III, by Group
- Value to Society. Mean Per Cent of Responses in Each Value Category, by Group
- The 10 Events Seen as Most Valuable to Society by Each Group

It is interesting to note that many of the tables found useful were not thought of before the data were being analyzed. The computer program cards for the analysis of the data were written in real-time according to the needs and interests of the users, something that would have been quite tedious without a simple language (APL) and an interactive terminal facility.

Conclusion

The purpose of this essay was to examine the use of computers in studying the future by looking at some ways in which computers are used for the manipulation of forecasting data.

Considering the capabilities of the computer for handling large amounts of information quickly and accurately, it is not surprising that planners are looking to it as a tool to aid them in their complex tasks of trying to have some idea of what the future is going to be like. Add to this the increasing accessibility of the computer, brought about by the development of time-sharing, remote access terminals, and simple, powerful programming languages, and it might seem surprising that planners do not make more use of computers than they do. One of the reasons more planners do not make greater use of computers is probably the same reason that a great deal of misuse is made of them, namely, the mystique that has inadvertently grown up about the machine and its power. The computer's power seems so great that people who know how to use it are assumed by others to possess an ability to accomplish extraordinary things.

While educators should certainly avail themselves of these tools for what they have to offer, they should not let the mystique of the machine nor the complexity of the model lead them to forget that the state of knowledge about most systems is such that reasonably comprehensive models are not yet possible. On the other hand, computer models, in their demand for explicitness, may prove extremely useful in forcing educators to think more clearly, and the computer's storage and retrieval capabilities can add a new dimension to the use of information about education, present and future.

Notes

(1) Paul Alper, "Some Considerations of Planning Engendered by Modern Control Theory" (Trondheim, Norway: Institut for Socialoconomi, Norges Tekniske Hogskole, 1971).

(2) J. C. Byrnes, *The Quantity of Formal Instruction in the United States* (Syracuse, N. Y.: Educational Policy Research Center, August 1969).

(3) For a more thorough discussion of the use of CIM, see T. Gordon, R. Rochberg and S. Enzer, *The Use of Cross-Impact Matrices for Forecasting and Planning* (Middletown, Conn.: Institute for the Future Report R-10, 1970).

(4) This stage of the exercise is quite similar to Sandow's Cross-Purpose Matrix. See Stuart A. Sandow, *Educational Policy Formulation: Planning with the Focus Delphi and Cross-Purpose Matrix* (Syracuse: Educational Policy Research Center, RR-9, March, 1972).

(5) A more comprehensive discussion of the problems of CIM can be found in M. J. Folk, *A Critical Look at the Cross-Impact Matrix* (Syracuse, N. Y.: Educational Policy Research Center, RR-5, August 1971).

(6) See Sandow, *Educational Policy Formulation.*

(7) Hudspeth, D. R., S. Sandow and D. Barclay, *A Long Range Planning Tool for Education* (Albany, N. Y.: New York State Education Dept., 1970).

VI

The Constraints of Language on Our Views of the Future: Experiments with Legal Issues in Education

Stuart A. Sandow

Early in the Fall of 1970 I stood talking with a group of law students at a major university in the East discussing their work on a law review. They described to me the work they did and the power they had over other reviews in the country. As a repository institution, they received decisions long before other schools did, and they noted that immediacy and relevance were the key problems in law review preparation. Their primary tasks were to comment on the emerging cases of the day.

I described the precedent-setting Marjorie Webster case to them and they found no excitement in the anti-trust issue. I posed a conjecture to them and said, "What if a student sued his school board for fraud?"

They responded, "There is no precedent for it." I went away.

Several weeks later in a similar gathering at the same school, I mentioned that the evening edition of a paper which I knew they could not have yet read detailed the fraud case described above as having occurred. I treated it as an occurred reality. I said that the paper in its incomplete style of reporting had omitted the arguments presented in the case. I asked the group for their estimates as to the positions of the two sides of the case. They were filled with ideas that would have been sufficient for the successful pursuit of the case only when they were convinced it had occurred and was done. They could then describe several strategies sufficient to cause its occurrence.

I told them I lied. They went away.

This experience proved to mark the end of a long period of reflection. The assumptions that underlie the work discussed below have to do with the nature of knowledge; how it is held, and its relationship to real time. Also with the nature of human deliberation;

what information or facts will be brought to bear and how different is the intellectual weight given to wishes, hopes and fears for the future balanced against knowledge from the past and immediate present.

The assumptions are that:

- During the period of time when a belief is held to be true, (i.e., is treated as knowledge) it has no time referent. When knowledge does not stand the test of time, those facts become time linked once again. They become once-upon-a-time facts, once-upon-a-time beliefs.

- There is a lack of full faith in intuitive assumptions and beliefs about the emerging future. They remain opinions; something less than knowledge. They either occur (if they are phenomena) or persist until the majority of men believe them to be true (if it is a model or theory of reality).

- Men are limited in these discussions about the future by the words they have to describe what they see. The future *is* the dark hole of the unknown not only because it has not been experienced but because its component parts cannot yet be named.

- In a similar sense the present, filled with all its components, each named, has not yet had a name attached to its whole. An age tends to be named only after it has passed. Usually the act of naming an age signals its end.

- The future then appears to be a place where one will know where he was—but not where he is, or where he is going.

- Individuals seem more willing to make statements and claims about the future if they think it already has occurred. When asked only to intuit future relationships they tend to freeze.

This report is a first cut at sharing work in progress on the nature of knowledge claims, the relationship between knowledge and time, and the impact of language on our deliberations.

The Issue:
Time-Linked Language

Policy analysis for the future is done by so-called experts for use by clients who request analysis, including the highest offices in the country. Advisement is an extremely tenuous role at best, and demands that the advisory group tap for expertise individuals whose knowledge or opinions can be trusted to be a valuable input to the policy process.

The way that individual experts are queried, the amount and kind of information they are given all act to filter their response. While policy issues always imply a concern with the future, we have very little practical knowledge about the effect of key variables on the way men do that deliberation. The fundamental problem addressed here is the impact of time-linked language on the way men respond to policy proposals when they act as expert advisors.

Because major policy issues that affect education sooner or later reach the courts and prompt legislative action, inquiries were made into the nature of the learning process of individuals who are prime actors in that milieu. Most of the nation's legislators have been trained in law. Every profession that continues through time develops habits. Habits are hard to break. The actions that comprise the habits come to be seen as necessary ways of behaving, thinking, or acting.

Law and Policy Process

Habits are broken when one conjectures about the future. Education in this society is a habit. So is Law. But the educational modes, and styles, the knowledge and truths and philosophies change daily.

The major upheavals in societies today are in many ways directly linked to education—a process not controlled by those who experience it or experienced by those who control it. The students of today are crying out with descriptions of alternative sufficient strategies of preparing themselves for the future and are met on every side by the strategies drawn from the past that are thought to be necessary, imposed on them by the education system.

One of the prime forces of social modification and change has been the effect of precedent case law. Many of the issues in those cases do not belong in the courts. Rather, the issues are the concern of the elected legislators charged with anticipating and serving the needs of multiple publics. But increasingly often citizens demand action faster than can be met through the political arena.

A fundamental problem is to identify emerging educational policy issues in law and prepare analysis of those issues for examination by legislators and educators early enough to allow adequate lead time for responsible decision making. The concern is with clarifying the form and content of information sufficient to impact on policy.

There are emerging in our society precedent cases that, successfully pursued through the courts, set the stage for still more change. These precedent cases can be conjectured about in the present to describe the probable and plausible actions that can be set in motion by further decisions. These can and should be studied as a resource for policy makers.

Elective offices at the federal and state level are, for the most part, filled with men whose formal educational experience includes some background in law. Legislators play a major role in defining the parameters of acceptable modes of behavior for the society. This point cannot be overlooked in discussions about policy and decision making which affect the future.

The rhetoric of futures thinkers has as one of its basic tenets that the future is filled with alternatives. It is held that the foreseen future can be described as an acceptable alternative to today and can be planned for by striving for certain ends to the deliberate exclusion of others. This assumes that, while no alternative is necessary, a rather wide range of alternatives are possible and policy can be designed to make them more probable. They may fill the spectrum from good to bad, but each is in turn sufficient as an acceptable future—each an alternative to the present.

To describe alternative futures one conjectures a state of affairs different from today. After locating that future in the continuum of times (past-to-future), one can describe the hypothetical minimum sufficient changes that must occur in order for the specified alternative future to occur. These are, in effect, a series of "if . . . then" propositions. By conjecture, men describe new relationships that might never have occurred in the past, in such a way as to demonstrate the plausibility of a future that is new or decidedly different than has ever been known. Conjecture is a leaping into the unknown with a tracing of strategic routes (or plans) back through time in order to describe how a specified future could come to be.

But when men analyze the past to demonstrate how things came to be, they do not conjecture, in this sense. Conjecture is intuitive and deals with the behaviors of men sufficient to reach an un-occurred future; extrapolation is reflective and deals with behaviors which once were really only sufficient, but have come to be seen as necessary by the very fact of their having occurred.

The law emphasizes the non-alternative past. The law draws its strength and power from the continuance of our past traditions into the future. Forecasting the future by describing analogies from the past excludes the impact of individual human beings and treats all mankind as constant through time, holding similar—never changing—beliefs, values, morals, and needs. What is addressed here is the mind set that considers the future in terms inconsistent with the rhetoric of alternative futures. The prescriptive power of law is not addressed.

The law is steeped in the past through the emerging history of cases. It depends on the continuance of belief in the meaning of right and wrong. But changes do occur. They occur regularly through various precedents. Often these precedent-setting cases are referred to as landmark decisions. What are landmark decisions or precedents? They are nothing more than sufficient alternative ways of describing the meaning of our world so that all that has come before is no longer necessarily correct. Further, they are the conjecture of one man representing another who believes there is an alternative, sufficient to substantiate his view.

Precedential cases change the shape and meaning of the society. They are as revolutionary in their long-range effects as are the actions of mobs and social class upheavals; but they have a unique distinction that should not be lost in this article. *Precedent setting cases are always actions of "one man vs. the past"—one man having an alternative sufficient perception of the meaning of his world.* In the United States alone, Escobedo, Brown, Kind, Serrano, Griggs, to name only a few, coupled with the actions of their counsel, describe to a world a state of affairs where their actions demand reassessment and are heard first in court, then throughout the land. It would appear that any decision of a court is not necessary, only sufficient. But over time these decisions, by repetition, come to be treated as necessary.

Focus: Emerging Legal Issues

With the support of the Educational Policy Research Center at Syracuse four explorations in emerging legal issues were carried out. The explorations help clarify and place in perspective emerging issues that face the United States. This work tries to identify the impact of changing realities on education. The work translates Center research into specific legal issues—issues that point up inequities in service or reveal policy alternatives. Here is listed in brief the nature of the inquiries.

- All the inquiries were prepared in the past tense; that is, people were never asked "what if . . ."; rather, the interviewer always began with a non-negotiable present; "Today, the 6th circuit court . . ."
- The respondents were not asked and were not given an opportunity to say "It can't happen;" rather, they were asked to describe their best estimates of the probable arguments that are sufficient to give the case a successful hearing.
- All questions were asked based on the existence of the decision. Not "can it happen?" but "how did it happen?"

For each issue addressed in the series, approximately 200 individuals were invited to respond to our inquiries. At least 90% of them were trained in law and included: chief state school officers, legislators in state and federal offices, university presidents, house counsel for major education corporation, deans of law schools, counsel for relevant public and private agencies, and law review editors.

The four issues examined to date, (1) presented in the form of invented news accounts, are as follows:

No. 1: *Fraud* (November 1970)
LaFayette School Board Guilty of Fraud
The Supreme Court today refused to hear an appeal from the Third Circuit Court in the case of John Brockman vs. The LaFayette Board of Education.

The case concerned the fact that while Brockman, 19, received a diploma from the LaFayette High School, he could only read at a seventh grade level.

His lawyers argued that the school system failed in its obligation to provide him with the learning skills they imply he received by awarding the diploma . . .

No. 2: *Career Obsolescence and Social Security* (April 1971)
'Obsoleted' Expert Eligible for Social Security Benefits!
Appeal Filed!!

PHILADELPHIA — The United States District Court in Philadelphia ruled today that John Aerosmith, an unemployed aerospace engineer, is eligible to receive advances, etc., from the social security trust fund.

Attorneys for the government have appealed to the United States Circuit Court of Appeals, and have indicated that, if the decision of the lower court is upheld, they will appeal to the Supreme Court.

No. 3: *Unequal Student Aid* (June 1971)
Unequal Student Aid Declared Unconstitutional!!!
Court decision will force legislative action

ALBANY — A New York State Supreme Court judge in Albany ruled today that the State must support equally all students attending any public or private institution of higher learning in the State. In the ruling, unequal support based upon the institution an individual attends, was declared unconstitutional, and the existing system was charged with creating a classification "which constitutes an invidious discrimination clearly denying equal protection under the law." . . .

No. 4: *Public-Private Competition in Higher Education* (July 1971)
State University Found Negligent!!!
Guilty of exceeding statutory authority

ALBANY — A New York State Supreme Court judge in Albany ruled today that the State University of New York had clearly exceeded its statutory authority under the New York Education Law, by offering curricula in excess of public demand at the expense of private institutions, and that their activities bordered on negligence. Judge S. B. Schroeder's ruling, directed to SUNY's Board of Trustees, ordered an immediate end to any curriculum currently offered which placed the State-supported campuses in direct competition with private colleges and universities where no real need exists. . . .

The significance of the ideas touched on here is that often language relationships are taken for granted or their impact ignored.

To study and examine a future, an individual must consider his examination as merely sufficient. When futurists sell educational policy-makers techniques that induce consensus, or conformity to an opinion, based on "knowledge" of the future, each individual's ability to believe is threatened. Those who disagree with the consensus find the foundation of all their questions about the future weak and undermined. Consensus attempts to induce closure. Too early closure compels us to operate as if what we do were necessary rather than merely sufficient, inevitable rather than a matter of choice.

Note

(1) The reports of this work are available from the Educational Policy Research Center at Syracuse, entitled *Emerging Educational Policy Issues in Law.*

Part Three

Applications of the Futures Perspective in Planning

VII

Converging Concerns
of Futurists and Planners:
Changing Viewpoints
in Educational Planning
in the OECD Area

Maureen M. Webster

Planners and futurists differ in their institutional base, their positions in relation to policy making, their perceived influence and accountability, the audiences they address, and the techniques and approaches they use in studying the future of education. There is some healthy skepticism on the part of planners about whether futurists can make a usable contribution to the practical problems of planning and on the part of futurists about the adequacy of traditional planning for examining issues in light of alternative futures. Yet traditional viewpoints in planning are undergoing significant change; and futures research is becoming increasingly policy oriented. Hence the focus of this essay upon converging concerns of planners and futurists.

*Shifting Viewpoints
in Planning, 1961-1970*

Changing viewpoints, of pivotal significance for planning in years ahead, can be traced in the documented experience of OECD-related planning groups in the 1960's. (1) The Organization for Economic Co-operation and Development (the OECD), by self-description, is "the world's largest grouping of industrialized market economy countries, comprising nineteen European nations, the United States,

Canada, and Japan, who work together for economic growth, aid to developing countries and expansion of trade." (2) The decade of the 'sixties was a time of major and influential OECD activity in the domain of educational planning, delimited by two major policy conferences. In October 1961, the Washington Policy Conference on Economic Growth and Investment in Education set the tone and perspectives for planned development of education in member countries and for their approach to assisting educational planning in the Third World. A decade later, the Paris Conference on Policies for Educational Growth, on the basis of extensive documentation of experience, examined the nature and consequences of past growth in education, took stock of current problems and presented new guidelines for policies and planning in the 1970's—guidelines reflecting significant departure from the prescriptions of the beginning of the decade. (3)

Why were new policy guidelines necessary? The years between the Washington and Paris policy conferences—the "decade of development"—witnessed the achievement and even surpassing of ambitious targets for overall economic growth and expansion of education in the OECD area. Yet papers of the 1970 Conference refer to past growth in education as a "runaway rather than a planned process" and speak of "substantial doubt about important aspects of our understanding about the role of education in society." The challenge to assumptions and perspectives which undergirded expansion policies in the 1960's derives from success and the consequences of success in achieving targets. That challenge has come from inside and outside planning circles and is reflected in shifting viewpoints concerning the overall context of planning, its content, its process, and its time horizon.

The Changing Context of Planning

Consider first changing views of economic growth and of the relationships between education and national development. The prime objective of the OECD is the promotion of sustained economic growth with high levels of employment. This has provided the rationale for OECD's activities in educational planning, which originated in the 1950's when European member countries initiated programs to meet shortages of skilled manpower considered necessary for the attainment of growth targets. In the early 1960's economic growth appeared to be viewed as the catalyst and reflector of human progress and well-being; the more of it the better for human welfare. Studies in the economics of education suggested that relative increases in investment in formal education would produce returns in the form of GNP growth rates. Moreover, in line with the prevalent growth-as-progress view, it seemed reasonable to assume that expansion of schooling would involve more equitable distribution of educational opportunities and thence of educational benefits in the form of life chances.

By the end of the decade these assumptions were increasingly recognized as tenuous; they do not hold unconditionally, and the conditions under which they might obtain are not yet known with assurance. Mounting evidence shows that growth is a mixed blessing and that it is not a synonym for social progress or human welfare. The adverse side effects of growth (notably environmental pollution and diminished quality of life for many people) have become a political, as well as an economic issue in many countries, requiring reappraisal of the relationship between economic growth and other human and societal purposes. As for social progress, growth of itself has not fulfilled the rising and changing expectations of many who aspire to be its beneficiaries. It has taken place without substantial effect upon some deep-rooted rigidities in social structures; its achievement does not in itself assure equitable distribution of its benefits (or dis-benefits). And what is broadly true of growth in national product is also the case for expansion of schooling. Data from country after country in the OECD area attest that the remarkable expansion of enrollments at post-compulsory levels of schooling after World War II has occurred without substantial narrowing of regional and group disparities in participation.

Several major policy-level statements at the end of the 1960's make it clear that economic growth is no longer to be seen as an end in itself, but rather as a means to increasing *"quality of life."* The shift in focus from growth as such to growth in the service of quality of life, associated as it is with marked attention to the long-term future, raises many questions. What kind of "more" is "better"? What is growth good for? What is quality-of-life? And who decides upon it? What goals, whose goals for society? What future, whose future? These and other questions derived from changed views of growth in relation to human well-being have implications for planning and policy in education, given the intricate web of interdependence characterizing complex social systems. Clearly, the context of educational planning is being redefined—and in ways which allow for contributions from the alternative futures perspective.

The Changing Focus of Planning

The second shift in viewpoint to be noted involves the planning agenda. The common nucleus of work of national educational planning teams set up within OECD programs involved determination—on the basis of varying sets of assumptions—of the output of all parts of the formal educational system over the ensuing ten to fifteen years, and assessment of the costs and expenditures entailed by differing projected targets. (4) Country planning documents of the 1960's typically reflect major efforts to make quantified forecasts of such categories as enrollments, transition rates and graduations; needs for buildings, teachers and equipment; costs and expenditures. The analysis stopped short of relating such categories to processes of human learning and development. It was in this sense para-educational—but considered adequate to form policies to achieve three "given" goals of planning: meeting manpower requirements of the economy, democratizing education by responding to social demand, and increasing system efficiency.

The challenge to the adequacy of assumptions concerning the appropriate focus of planning has come both from inside and outside technical planning circles. In the second half of the decade there is some evidence within planning programs of shifts in understanding of given goals. For example, democratizing education is increasingly seen as requiring attention not just to opportunity for access (involving provision of places) but also to opportunity for achievement (involving concern for learning environments and processes). Research and development, innovation, the knowledge-practice gap in education more frequently enter discussion towards the end of the 1960's—a shift in emphasis supported by the establishment in 1968 of OECD's Centre for Educational Research and Innovation.

The major impetus accelerating attention to education itself—its purposes and clientele as well as its processes—has come from outside professional planning groups in the form of student unrest, teacher militancy and active community disenchantment with education. In the last years of the 'sixties close examination of educational processes (often previously ignored) and purposes (previously taken as given) became politically, as well as economically and educationally, imperative. The "relevance crisis" has propelled recognition that para-educational analysis of the how-many-how-much-what-cost variety is a necessary but not a sufficient basis for decision-making concerning the future of education. Planning must now seek to address questions about education itself: what it is for, whom it is for, and where, when and how it takes place.

The Changing Locus of Planning

Planning has traditionally been considered a specialized technical activity, to be performed by experts (often economists). Planning groups typically have been centralized close to government decision makers (considered political) who utilize planners' analyses (assumed to be apolitical) to "make policy." But the reasonableness of these views has also been questioned. The locus and nature of planning is a third area in which there are significant changes in viewpoint.

In the late 'sixties conventional assumptions about the nature and locus of planning in relation to decision making were severely challenged by interest groups in the polity who refused to be excluded from processes by which their future is invented. In 1968 that challenge came to a head in many countries, particularly in universities, generating crises which planning had not anticipated and was unprepared to deal with. The "relevance crisis" (education for what?) is intricately interwoven with the participation crisis (who shall decide?). The first reflects dissatisfaction with the performance of education in relation to multiple and changing social goals; the second attests dissatisfaction with decision making processes whereby ends and means are chosen. It is clear that if planning is to be relevant, it must satisfy at least three conditions. First, it must examine ends as well as means. Second, it must be integrated in the decision making process. Third, it must be open to participation by multiple publics in the polity of education—that is, by those affected by it. Such a shift in views of planning is confirmed in the papers and conclusions of the 1970 Policy Conference.

The heavy emphasis upon participation raises further questions. What is the nature of the process of policy planning in particular politico-cultural environments? Who is to participate, at what levels, in what activities within that process? What kinds of capacities, information and communication will have to be developed to facilitate and enable meaningful participation? What are to be the roles and functions of professional planners in a participatory planning process?

The Changing
Time Dimension in Planning

Finally, we may note an extension of the time horizon in national planning, associated with the quality-of-life context identified above.

At the end of the 'sixties such documents as the Bellagio Declaration on Planning (1968), the Economic Outlook Report (1970), the Statement of the OECD Council of Ministers (1970) all attest serious concern for broader and longer-term planning perspectives and increased attention to planning policy interventions to curb the likelihood of less favored futures (diminished quality of life) and to enhance the possibility of more desirable futures (increased quality of life). Many member governments are embarking upon "perspective planning" as a context for shorter-term decision making; this has generated demands for long-term planning in the education sector among others.

Planning Redefined, 1970

The broader and longer-term perspectives for general socio-economic planning at the national level are reflected in the four-point prescriptive definition of educational planning presented in the Conclusions of the 1970 Conference: (5)

Now, more than ever, educational planning must be *long-term, comprehensive, integrated* with general economic and social policy, and *overall* in the sense that it must embrace all educational activities both formal and informal.

Moreover, "the process of choice among [alternative policies] should be the occasion for the widest possible participation and discussion."

This definition of educational planning is not a statement of what is, but of what "must be." Its full implications—conceptual, methodological, substantive, operational—have yet to be elaborated. The 1970 guidelines suggest that "planners should present an analysis of alternative policies for education based on explicit goal formulation, with short- and long-term consequences for the individual, the educational system, the economy and society as a whole." Here again changing viewpoints generate a series of questions. Where shall we find the information, logic, techniques and methods to undertake these analyses of goals, means, policies, consequences, performance? How shall we develop and disseminate the capacities to engage in these kinds of analyses? And, given emphasis upon the long-term time period, how shall we plan such that we avoid colonizing the future with the past and present, but rather leave some meaningful alternatives open for those who will inhabit the future? The task is awesome. Past modes of planning are quite inadequate to it. The new imperatives of planning require drawing upon a much wider range of fields of study and insight than have been tapped thus far.

The Futures Perspective
and the Planning Agenda

An Agenda of Questions

Consider Table 3 which assembles documented shifts in viewpoint regarding the context, content, locus and time dimension of planning, together with some fundamental questions which they raise. Taken together, these changes and questions have a cumulative, synergistic effect, forcing attention to a set of issues to be addressed if planning and policy are to be more adequate than in the past to the task of guiding and facilitating action towards multiple educational/societal goals, encompassed in the phrase "quality of life." Taken together, their interdependence becomes evident. They involve overall social change and a policy planning process intended to serve it—not education in isolation, but the future of education as it is imbedded in society at a time when there are strong currents of change in both.

The convergence of interests of futurists and planners arises from the nature of the issues now being raised—on the one hand out of planning experience, and on the other out of futures studies and research. That elements of the futures perspective are already implanted in planning discussion and activities is evidenced in the records of OECD initiatives in the second half of 1960's—both in the area of science and technology and in education. The concept of alternative educational futures is explicitly incorporated and

TABLE 3

Changing Viewpoints in Educational Planning
in the OECD Area, 1960-1970

A. Area of change	B. Direction of change		C. Agenda of questions, circa 1970
	From	To	
Planning context	Economic growth	→ Quality of life	What kind of more is better for whom? What goals for society? Whose goals? What future? Whose future?
Content & analysis	Para-educational categories	→ Learning and change processes	What education? For whom? Where? When? How?
Planning/policy relationships	Planning as a technical, value-free activity, segregated from policy-making	Planning involving questions of choice and values, and part of a policy-planning process	Who is to participate? In what process/activities? On what grounds? By what means?
Locus of planning activity	Planning by centralized professional groups	→ Participatory planning by multiple publics	
Time horizon	Short-to-medium range planning	→ Long-term perspective planning	How shall we view the future in planning for education/ quality of life? What time perspective can illumine questions of planning context, content, and process?

elaborated in the documents of the 1970 Conference. (6) At the present time, in addition to innovative analysis within individual countries and planning agencies, several member countries are cooperating in joint policy research through the OECD—including in-depth examination of policies for "recurrent education" and development of "second generation educational planning," in which alternative educational futures are being explored. Some inroads are thus already being made on the agenda of questions.

The Futures Perspective

Given the propensity of traditional planning to deal with the future in largely extrapolative terms (imposing past and present upon the future) or as a unidimensional variation of the present (some aspects of society conceived to change, all other aspects assumed constant), it is well to review the features of the futures perspective. For a time horizon (the number of years ahead one attends to) is not the same thing as a time perspective (the way in which we view the future, or the present as seen from the future). The futures perspective insists upon *comprehensiveness*—upon confronting the *interdependencies* of educational/societal issues; upon attention to *alternatives,* in ends and means, in the present and for the future; and upon a *questive approach* to policy planning—seeking to keep the future open. It is the questive approach which insists upon transforming the conclusions about changed viewpoints in planning into questions forming a next-order agenda for action, rather than into definitive prescriptions likely to be weighted with unexamined assumptions.

The questive approach also characterizes the planning methods associated with the futures perspective. These involve readiness to engage in futures-casting as well as forecasting—mental movement back and forth across the territory of the future, which Warren L. Ziegler has aptly termed *ends-means/means-consequences analysis* and which Stuart A. Sandow has elaborated as a process for defining sufficient futures. (7) This distinctive form of reasoning requires casting forward in time to conjecture systematically about alternative possible future states, for each of which one then identifies multiple sufficient conditions at prior time periods back to the present (ends → means); and thinking forward through time to consider multiple consequences of chosen activities and strategies (means → consequences).

Assuming integrity of commitment to act in accord with articulated changes in viewpoint, we may posit that action towards quality of life goals is likely to be more effective to the extent that major issues are clearly identified and that capacities are developed to address them in a continuing process of policy planning. The futures perspective and the search and research with which it is associated can contribute to both tasks. It can both elucidate the planning agenda (an agenda which it formulates as questions) and inform the process in which that agenda is addressed (a process which it suggests is essentially questive). Therein lies the high potential of the futures perspective to aid those having the will to make the transition from deepened insight to transformation of planning as a guide to social choice and action.

A Global Enterprise

This brief account of issues confronting and being addressed in educational planning today in a number of developed countries has suggested a convergence of interests of futurists and planners and noted the actual and potential inputs of the futures perspective to addressing those issues. Yet, despite the international flavor of the account, a fundamental international dimension has been missing from discussion. It may be brought out by reference to a statement supported by some 150 educational leaders representing 52 countries (in nonofficial capacity) at the 1967 Williamsburg Conference on the World Crisis in Education. (8)

There is indeed a crisis in education's ability to match performance with expectations. The crisis takes two forms. The first is the world-wide disparity between the hopes of individuals and the needs of society, on the one hand, and, on the other, the capabilities of the educational system. The second is an even greater disparity between the developing countries, faced with the cruel restraints of grossly inadequate resources, and the developed countries, which are increasingly preoccupied with their own internal needs.

The OECD's 1961 Washington Conference addressed itself to problems of educational development in the Third World as well as in its member countries; the 1970 Paris Conference did not. But the futures perspective is no respecter of countries. It does not permit us the luxury of preoccupation only with our own internal needs. It calls, as did the Williamsburg Conference, for recognition that "education has become a global enterprise—a matter of mutual concern and mutual dependence involving literally all nations. United, the nations of the world can bring under control the educational crisis which affects them all. Divided it is most unlikely that they can do so."

What future, whose future? Education for what purposes, for whom, where, when, how? Who shall decide the answers to those questions, in what process, on what grounds, by what means? These questions are a universal, continuing agenda for planning. Unless the interdependencies of these questions and issues at the global level are confronted, efforts to revitalize processes and strategies of planning in the 'seventies will fall short of their claimed purpose: to promote quality of life. This global dimension of the new look in planning may well by the key test of whether the alternative futures perspective is to be internalized in planning activities of the developed countries—or whether nationalist constraints will set limits to the convergence of concerns of planners and futurists.

Notes

(1) This essay is based on in-depth appraisal of the evolution of educational planning in OECD Member programs in the 1960's using extensive published and unpublished documentation. A detailed exposition is presented in: Maureen Webster, *Educational Planning in Transition—Emerging Concerns and the Alternative Futures Perspective* (Syracuse: EPRC, 1971). (Restricted distribution). The proliferation of educational planning activities in the 1960's world-wide is evidenced in the explosion of literature for the period. See: Maureen Webster, *Educational Planning in the 'Sixties: An International Bibliography* (Syracuse: DPRC, 1972).

(2) Member countries of the OECD are: Austria, Belgium, Canada, Denmark, Finland, France, Germany (F.R.), Greece, Iceland, Ireland, Italy, Japan, Luxembourg, Norway, Netherlands, Portugal, Spain, Sweden, Switzerland, Turkey, United Kingdom, United States. Australia and Yugoslavia are special status Members. The OECD derives from the Organization for European Economic Co-operation and Development, established to promote economic recovery in Europe following the second world war.

(3) The papers of the 1961 conference are available as: OECD, *Policy Conference on Economic Growth and Investment in Education* (Paris: OECD, 1965—one volume edition). The major background studies of the 1970 conference have not yet been published (February 1972), but an exposition of policy guidelines is available as: OECD, *Educational Policies for the 1970's. General Report* (Paris: OECD, 1971).

(4) I have elsewhere critically examined the major approaches to educational planning—reflected in OECD documents among others. See: *Three Approaches to Educational Planning* (Syracuse: Syracuse University, Center for Development Education, 1970).

(5) Quotes are from paragraphs 35-36 of the mimeographed Conference Conclusions, which include the emphases. See also p. 143 of the published *General Report*.

(6) Note the work sponsored by OECD's Committee on Science Policy, including a commissioned study—Erich Jantsch, *Technological Forecasting in Perspective* (Paris: OECD, 1967); and a symposium on long-range forecasting and planning—Erich Jantsch, ed., *Perspectives of Planning* (Paris: OECD, 1969). In education, "alternative futures" entered the formal meetings of country planning groups at the 1969 session on long-range planning—with informal exchanges between planners and futurists before that time. CERI's work in educational futures led to a major background study for the 1970 conference: *Alternative Educational Futures in the United States and Europe: Methods, Issues, and Policy Relevance* (Paris: OECD, 1970. Restricted distribution). This includes papers by Torsten Husen, Warren Ziegler, and Willis Harman, with an introductory paper by CERI personnel.

(7) See: Warren L. Ziegler, "Some Notes on How Educational Planning in the United States Looks at the Future," *Notes on the Future of Education (EPRC/Syracuse), 1:1, 1:2, 1:3, 1969-1970. Also: Stuart A. Sandow, The Pedagogical Structure of Methods of Thinking about the Future* (Syracuse: EPRC, 1970). Working Draft.

(8) A book, elaborating the basic paper of the Williamsburg Conference, is: Philip H. Coombs, *The World Educational Crisis* (New York: Oxford University Press, 1968). The "Epilogue" of this volume is the Summary Report of the Conference Chairman—from which quotes in the present essay are drawn.

VIII

Can the Federal Government Use the Futures Perspective?

Hendrik D. Gideonse

At this writing exactly one year has passed since I left the United States Office of Education. My responsibilities in the research planning post I held there led to the conception, planning, establishment, and support of the first systematic attempts to project and study long-range educational futures as a support to policy development.

My present assessment of this attempt is that it has yet to succeed in any direct sense. It would not be possible to point to any present national education policies which have been affected by any of the futures research conducted by the two centers supported to carry out such work. The reasons for this circumstance lie in flaws in the present structure for education policy development at the federal level, in the character of the incentives which operate on the principal actors there, and in rather fundamental disagreements about what Washington's role ought to be or can be in making various different kinds of policy judgments bearing on education.

In July, 1965, I became the first Director of Planning for the old USOE Bureau of Research. It took several months to settle the programs down, but late in 1965, when Associate Commissioner R. Louis Bright first appeared on the scene, it became time to look seriously at what research planning might mean. One of the first propositions to strike us forcefully was that whatever decisions we made regarding research and development expenditures and allocations would not bear fruit for a considerable span of time. As we considered that point, a second proposition took on weight. To the extent that research produced the knowledge base from which future technical innovations might be derived, the areas in which we chose to invest for research would tend to determine the range of technical options that might be available in the future. Different research choices, in short, invented rather different future capabilities.

The research planning effort was launched as a result of our firm belief in the validity of those two propositions. It was something of a triumph in rational policy development. The planning effort was aimed at developing mechanisms to support the study of futures bearing on education. Present-day choices about what kinds of research and development activities to support might then be taken within a frame of reference that embraced what could be responsibly projected, analyzed, and synthesized respecting the future.

Together with Dr. David Goldberg and Dr. Dale Mann, a program development effort was launched by the planning staff. We read extensively in futures research. We traveled across the nation talking to practitioners of futures research about the feasibility of doing such work in education. We talked to educators about the need and the mechanisms by which such research might be conducted and used. We also initiated rather extensive discussions with our planning colleagues in Washington respecting their interest in participating with us on such a venture to share costs and outcomes.

Our conversations and study told us that, save for an individual here or there, no continuing group study efforts had yet been mounted systematically to explore education futures. On the other hand, we became convinced that only money and time needed to be applied to bring such activities into existence. Furthermore, the more we talked with educators and futures researchers, the more quickly it became apparent that there was intense scholarly and policy interest in beginning and continuing studies of educational futures.

Back in Washington, the three of us awakened strong interest in the planning staffs of other federal agencies, including the Secretary's planning staff in HEW, the National Institute of Mental Health, the Office of Economic Opportunity, the Department of Labor, the National Bureau of Standards, and others. Because of the complex, interlinked character of futures research for any area on which one might wish to focus, we believed that we might be able to interest several agencies in combining resources to produce a larger mass of funds that would assure that the maximum number of factors possible might be considered as the futures research was undertaken.

We were not mistaken as to the interest, but we were to be sadly disappointed when it came to matching the interest with an investment. Finally, at a multi-agency meeting called at our request by John Macy, Chairman of the Civil Service Commission, we were finally advised by Macy that if we had the money set aside, we ought to go ahead on our own rather than wait any longer for our sister agencies to make up their minds whether they wanted in or not.

Five pilot projects were supported in 1967, and in the spring of 1968 the two most promising of these were selected to become centers for the study of educational futures. With the naming of the program, however, we made our first compromise. Rather than call them simply Centers for the Study of Education Futures, after some soul-searching and after a thorough exploration of our fears that others might see such research as too "far out," we decided to call them Educational Policy Research Centers. Retrospectively, that compromise was our first mistake.

The second mistake we made was not to fulfill the side of the bargain we made with ourselves, with the Bureau's Research Advisory Council which approved the program finally after many policy presentations and much back and forth debate, and with the winning centers. When we were doing the planning for education futures research we early determined they would have little effect unless an interfacing futures research and interpretation capability was created within the Office of Education. That capability was never created.

The two centers are now more than four years old. Their impact on education may be assessed in three ways. If one should ask how have they affected individuals it is possible to point to a fairly large number and say the impact was great and perhaps even in a few instances profound. If one were to ask instead how have the centers affected other institutions besides the Office of Education, it is possible to point to an increasing number of specific cases and institutions at the state and local level and say that their impact has been quite direct and promising.

For example, the Skyline Alternative High School in Oakland, California, found the Alternative Futures and Educational Policy document of the Stanford Center one of the most influential source materials for curriculum planning. Prescott College in Arizona has worked closely with people from the Stanford Center to develop a futures curriculum. Several State Education Departments have been affected, as for example the Syracuse Center's work with the New York State Education Department on analyzing and assessing future developments, prospects and policy needs in post-secondary education. The Syracuse Center has also developed long-term educational design strategies and goals for a New Town (Gananda), near Rochester, N. Y.

But if one asks what affect can be seen on the Office of Education and on federal education policy, the answer must be very little. Why is this so? Why have the centers, almost from their inception, been the subject of veiled and not-so-veiled attacks and threats? Why may OE abandon the support of systematic efforts to project alternative futures for education?

A first, but only partial explanation, is to be found in the first compromise respecting the program, namely, the decision to call the centers for such work *policy* centers. In the narrow frame of reference within which Washingtonians revel, the word policy has a here and now cast to it which virtually proscribes looking at anything further ahead than eighteen months. Hence from their inception those responsible for managing the centers for OE were pressured to have them working on specific policy issues confronting the United States Office of Education. On occasion this preoccupation with near-time policy concerns even led to queries as to why, if the Centers were doing policy research, they were not actively engaged in the evaluation of ongoing federal or state educational programs!

Of course, the word "policy" cannot bear responsibility in and of itself, but it does provide a useful symbol to illustrate a larger problem. A second reason for lack of impact of the futures perspective in the Office of Education is the incompatibility of the operating incentives for key officials in the United States Office with the patterns and habits of thought characteristic of the futures perspective.

Of first importance in explaining this incompatability is the psychological time frame within which, consciously or unconsciously, key USOE officials operate. My tenure, for example, lasted six and a half years. During that time five men served as Commissioner or Acting Commissioner of Education. During the same period of time seven men served as Associate Commissioner or Acting Associate Commissioner for Research. Throughout government the average tenure of an Assistant Secretary is less than twenty-three months. With each new man comes a new set of priorities, a profound desire to accomplish something significant, and a period of substantial upheaval. None of these circumstances are especially conducive to the kind of work which aims at the patient systematic exploration of the linkages between policy options, the likely primary, secondary, and tertiary outcomes of those options, the attention to consequences over long periods of time, and the alterations in context surrounding implemented policies which are likely to occur and which are likely to drastically alter program consequences.

A third explanation for the failure of the futures perspective to affect the work of the Office of Education lies in the lack of understanding of key OE and HEW personnel of what futures research is, how it could come to affect policy, and what its implications are for the way in which OE and HEW like to view their role in the generation and implementation of educational policy in the Nation. These matters are complex and could be a subject of extensive discussion in their own right. Suffice it to say here that the idea of futures research being most important for the processes of thought and policy development which it engenders, rather than for the specific answers which it might provide, is not appreciated at all. Couple this misunderstanding with arrogance of bright young policy analysts who are here today and gone tomorrow pursuing their misbegotten belief that there are indeed objective answers to essentially subjective, political issues and the picture becomes even more clear. The finishing touches can then be added by noting the captivating temptation to believe in Washington, that the Capital is where policy really is supposed to be made for the rest of the nation (as contrasted, say, to explored, or facilitated, or illuminated). Since one of the clear messages arising from futures research applied to social and domestic problems is the need to cope more effectively with the emerging efficaciousness of pluralistic values in our society, it is not surprising that such a message would be virtually unhearable in an agency which behaves on the basis of almost exactly contradictory assumptions. Numerous critics of USOE (incorrectly, in my judgment) see it as an agency staffed by the largest collection of incompetents ever assembled under the pretense of being a professional agency. But, in fact, OE *behaves* as if it either knows or is in a position to know better than anyone else in the country what the best solutions are for curing the educational ills of the Nation. In short, its posture is basically elitist in character. Insofar as it is, OE simply does not hear messages that would require it to be something else or which are aimed directly at the monopoly of policy power which it would like to see itself wielding.

Finally, there is a fourth reason why national education policies have been unaffected by the futures work supported by OE. That is quite simply that OE is not the place where education policy is made in the executive branch. In fact, such policy is made in HEW and in the White House, and, if not there, in the education panels of the Office of Science and Technology or in the Office of Management and Budget. The counter argument that had good policies been proposed by OE, then that is where policy would have been made—in other words, that OE wasn't the place where policy was made because we made poor policy that had to be superceded by the work of other agencies—assumes a rational basis to policy development that any sensitive observer would have to deny. Policy development turns out to be far more often a matter of squeaky wheels, personality, and sheer political opportunism (certainly not always partisan, either), although on the margins it is possible for the application of logic and reason to have some effect.

All of this must sound pretty dismal. It should, for that is the way policy development in OE now takes place and why the futures perspective, as a special activity which has somehow to be grafted on because it is not yet integral to the policy view of the principal operatives, has so far had very little impact on national educational policy.

Paradoxically, the futures perspective will not have any effect on national policy until it has some. It is a kind of chicken/egg problem. Until it is there, it won't be. Of course, the chicken/egg problem isn't difficult for anyone to solve once they understand genetics and how chickens come about. In this case the egg must come in the form of choosing senior officials for OE who have that perspective and who demand its application in the generation, consideration, and choice from among ranges of policy options aimed at resolving the issues which they confront at any given point in time. The only way any policy tool will find shelter in an organization and give sustenance to the policy process is if the official making the choices knows and understands its value and insists upon its application. There is one other way such a tool finds its way into the policy process. It is sometimes possible for the people using the tool to intimidate their superiors, but such relationships in large bureaucracies are neither fruitful nor lasting. The choice of officials already having and appreciating the futures perspective is the only way, internally, it will be applied to the policy analysis, development, and implementation within the executive branch.

There are ways, however, in which the perspective can come to impinge on national education policy from the outside. One is the classic route through the ballot, by the election of Congressmen and Senators responsive to this view and by the shaping of their platforms and views in the manner that some of us from time to time are privileged to perform. A second is through the independent critical application of that perspective to national education issues as they arise by any of us who are around to do it. The generation of responsive debate and discussion back to the policy apparatus may, over time, force it to take such views into account.

Finally, there is a third way in which the futures perspective can (and in the final analysis *will*) finally impinge itself on national education policy. That is from the bottom up, from the thousands of young people and educators who have begun to understand how little time remains to mankind to resolve very big questions raised by all the forces behind social and technological change, and who, realizing that education is nothing if it is not for those who are engaged in it and particularly those who by law are required to be formally engaged upon it, understand that thirty-year time frames for policy development, from the eyes of a fifteen-year old young lady reach barely half way through her adult life.

This grassroots approach, the development of courses of instruction under the leadership of people like Billy Rojas and Mark Markley or spontaneously by young people themselves, is likely to have over the long run a far more profound impact on national education policy than any direct application on a particular policy could hope to have.

A final note about the morality of applying the futures perspective to national education policy. One of the reasons the futures perspective is not now applied to education policy is that there is no organized constituency behind it. When we think of it that way, however, it is possible to see the absence of the application of the futures perspective as one more piece of evidence of the extent to which educational policy disenfranchises and oppresses the young. Formal education is and for a long time to come will be primarily for the young. Being so, it is also for the future. Being so, we oppress the young when we operationally choose not to apply the futures perspective policy analysis in this field. The aims and goals and objectives of youth and the many environments which will surround their lives in the future must be consciously brought to bear upon the choice of education policies and the realization of the goals and objectives of education. This is what will distinguish us as professionals, finally, when we take our clients' interests as primary and ours as secondary. One important sign that we have done this will be the general application of the futures perspective to educational policy wherever it is considered.

IX

Comprehensive Statewide Planning: The Promise and the Reality

Edgar L. Morphet,
David L. Jesser,
and Arthur P. Ludka

Planning means many things to many people. It is virtually impossible to find anyone—especially in education—who would be willing to admit that he or she does not plan. Everyone plans—but all too often he plans to do tomorrow what he did yesterday. Relatively few people have made any serious effort to consider what a future situation will probably be like, and to choose rationally between reasonable and practical alternatives that can be identified.

Growing Insights and Concern

Within recent years, however, there has been increasing concern—among educators and others alike—about more effective ways of bringing about educational change. Major thrusts in this type of effort have been made by projects such as *Designing Education for the Future, Comprehensive Planning in State Education Agencies,* and *Improving State Leadership in Education.* (1) Additional impetus has been provided by many other educational leaders, and has been typified by the emerging concepts of *planning for change, strategies for change, strategies for educational improvement, dynamics of change,* and *systematic planning.*

The need for systematic and continuous long-range planning for effecting improvements in education is currently receiving more consideration, and gaining more acceptance than ever before. There is a growing recognition of the fact that although change will take place whether or not we prepare for it, *appropriate planning can help to offset many of the difficulties that may result from unanticipated change.* Through comprehensive planning, "blue sky" and "top of the head" decisions can be minimized and adjustments can often be made before problems become serious.

Planning as a Process

There are many definitions and models of planning. But however it is defined, and however the model is structured, planning—properly interpreted—is basically a systematic process wherein it is possible to ascertain *where we are, where we want to go, and how we might get there.* It is a process, a means of identifying and achieving some appropriate goal or goals. *The process is the most important concomitant of comprehensive educational planning.*

Primarily because many of the major environmental, social and other problems that society faces extend beyond established boundaries in jurisdiction, scope and responsibility of existing systems, it is not possible for a single individual, group, institution or agency to provide the needed expertise or resources to cope successfully with these problems. *Educational planning, therefore, cannot be isolated from other developments in the cultural, economic, and political aspects of the social system.*

Planning for and effecting needed educational change is not an easy process. Educational decisions in a state, for example, may be made by the Governor, the legislature, the voters, the state board of education, the chief state school officer and the governing boards and administrative officers of the local education agencies. Students, parents, other concerned lay citizens, teachers, local and state agencies, and institutions provide the inputs, on the basis of which the educational decisions are made, and thus are important factors in this process.

Meaningful Involvement

The need for meaningful involvement of people in the change process has been expressed in a variety of ways by any number of leading educators. Fundamentally, however, most of the thoughts seem to be centered around the relationship between *understanding* and *acceptance* of change.

The idea that people will accept and support change to the degree that they understand the reason, or need for change has been suggested by Edgar L. Morphet:

. . . significant changes in instruction and learning are likely to be made only when the need and the importance are recognized and understood by those involved. (2)

In another, but similar context, Morphet stressed the need for involvement:

Unless citizens understand the *need* for making changes, and are convinced that these changes will result in the *improvement* of education, the changes are not likely to be made. (3)

From the preceding thoughts there are two rather basic assumptions that can be made about people and change:

- People must understand the reason or purpose of a proposed change before they can be expected to accept or support it.
- When people participate in the change process (including *planning* for the change) they are more likely to be supportive of the change than when they do not.

Interrelationship of Parts

Perhaps one of the most widely used and least understood terms currently in vogue with educators relates to the system approach to planning. Some educators, in bandwagon fashion, accept the term without question because "others have found the approach to be successful." Others reject the approach because "it is new, and may not work." Both attitudes portrayed are unfortunate, because *a system approach,* as in any good planning, *is capable of making valuable contributions to the solution of problems so long as it incorporates the concepts of structure, whole, the relationship of parts to each other, and of parts to a whole.*

Essentially, a system approach to planning or problem-solving consists of the three identifiable basic components that are illustrated in the following diagram:

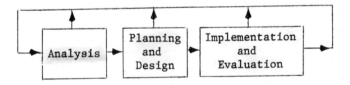

Obviously, there are an almost infinite number of variations, but they will always be variations on the same theme.

The Promise

During and even prior to the 1920's, a number of states and local school systems contracted with outside "experts" and organizations to make surveys or studies and prepare reports. Some were concerned with long- as well as short-range proposals, while others dealt primarily with what were defined as urgent problems or "crisis" situations. The emphasis, however, seemed to be on the use of outside "experts."

Significant Developments

In the early 1940's many people and organizations began to express doubts about the use of studies and reports by outside "experts" as the best approach to the solution of many problems in education. They pointed out that even the best plans or proposed solutions for social problems are not likely to be accepted by people who have not been involved in the studies or in developing the plans or proposals. Some of these concepts were incorporated in proposals made by important groups:

In 1944, the Council on Chief State School Officers stated that:

The planning procedure and process should be carefully formulated, unified, and systematically carried out.

Definite provision for planning must be made in educational organizations in order that planning may proceed satisfactorily and attain tangible results.

Educational planning to be functional must be realistic and practical but should not be needlessly limited by existing situations.

All educational planning should involve the active and continuing participation of interested groups and organizations. (4)

In 1945, the Southern States Work Conference on Educational Problems made the following observations:

More attention should be given to the development of comprehensive and well integrated plans (for the improvement of education).

Planning should be projected in terms of the aims (and goals) of education and of society and therefore must take into consideration the (needs and interests of all) groups in the planning area. (5)

In a report published in 1967, the International Institute for Educational Planning, created by UNESCO, commented:

In the past decade a new kind of educational planning has become necessary to cope with the sweeping changes in education's environment and with the vastly accelerated pace of change and growth in education itself. (6)

In 1965, the project, Designing Education for the Future, was organized to:

Assist the people in each of the eight participating states (in the Rocky Mountain and Great Basin area) to anticipate the changes that are likely to take place in this country, in the region served by the project, and within each of the states participating in the project during the next ten to fifteen years, and to plan and implement changes and improvements that should be made in the educational organization and program during that period. (7)

The procedures utilized to accomplish the broad goals of the Designing Education for the Future project incorporated elements considered to be essential for *effective* planning. There was a broad-based *involvement* of people in the various committees that were organized and in the conferences that were held. Through this type of *people involvement,* and by utilizing information that was provided in the form of narrated filmstrips, publications and consultants, it was possible for most of the participating states to obtain agreement as to goals of education, and to begin to develop plans for attaining them.

Important Perceptions

There are always some people who believe that planning for improvements in education may ultimately result in a planned society, or in an educational program blue-printed by planning experts who rely on automated machines that provide "the answers." However, as pointed out by the Designing Education for the Future project, there is a vast difference between a *planned society* and a *planning society*.

In the planning process there are appropriate roles and procedures for various kinds of experts and specialists, for educators and for lay citizens, and for the use of computers and other machines and their products. The planning experts and other appropriate specialists—utilizing any tools or machines they find helpful—may assemble and analyze data, make projections, identify feasible alternative goals and procedures and ascertain *the implication of each alternative.* However, they should not attempt to determine either the choices to be made or the basic actions to be taken. *These decisions must be made by the people or their representatives* who are responsible for determining the basic policies for education.

The *cooperative* approach to planning in education is essential. In technical areas or aspects of education, qualified educators—with appropriate assistance by recognized leaders—can and should develop and lead in implementing plans. But in terms of basic policy decisions the people involved must reach substantial agreement before any such policy can be adopted or implemented. Cooperative planning will tend to facilitate understanding, wise decisions and effective implementation.

A Continuing Dilemma: The Reality

There are many educators who seem to believe that, because change is inevitable and *will* take place, their primary task is one of waiting until it is possible to ascertain the direction of the change that is taking place, and then determining how best to adapt to it. In effect, such educators are content with "riding with the current." Such efforts would be analogous to those of a sailor who determined which way the wind was blowing before deciding upon his destination. They are representative of the many educators who apparently are content to be influenced by change, but who are either unwilling or unable to engage in the process of *influencing* change.

Apparent inadequacies in the planning role of state and local education agencies have been pointed out quite clearly for at least the last quarter of a century. For example, the Southern States Work

Conference on School Administrative Problems in 1945, clearly recognized not only the inadequacies but also the need for change to be made. The Conference Report stated that:

Changes in economic, political, and social life and changes in the conception of the functions of education now place responsibilities on educational agencies not formerly anticipated. The need for careful planning in education has, as a result, been greatly accentuated. Continuous planning is essential if education is to meet changing needs. (8)

The picture of planning at the state level, however, is not entirely negative. The Fourth Annual Report of the Advisory Council on State Departments of Education (9) for example, indicates that state education agencies are developing an awareness of the need and are beginning to take steps to provide leadership in educational planning. With the assistance of federal funds and by utilizing limited state funds, some state education agencies are developing a bona fide planning competence. The progress achieved in Colorado, Florida, Nevada, Texas, Utah, Vermont, and Virginia, for example, has been reported in several case studies sponsored by the Improving State Leadership in Education project. (10) These and other developments reinforce the point of view that *the state is the logical entity to coordinate the piecemeal and compartmentalized planning that is prevalent in much of education.*

But while the promise that comprehensive planning holds for state education agencies is attaining a higher degree of clarity, the reality is that fundamental and basic problems still exist in such agencies. Problems such as the following were listed by states participating in the Designing Education for the Future project as being of major importance:

- They are asked to make changes of all types without clear rationale for such changes.
- There is an absence of criteria to guide them after the reasons are established.
- Educators have too little evidence to help them to know the directions of change in society.
- Too little is known of the implications of social change for schools and departments of education.

The Need for Effective Planning

The urgent need for meaningful and responsive changes in the existing educational system has been well documented. Moreover, the necessity for more adequate and effective planning for urgently needed changes in education has also been well documented. However, even though these needs have been recognized by educational leaders for many years, concerned citizens—educators, legislators and lay citizens—are becoming increasingly aware of the fact that *relatively few meaningful and lasting changes have occurred in education.*

More students have been enrolled, more classroom units have been created, more teachers have been hired, more buildings have been built, and more curriculums have been added. These, of course, constitute certain kinds of changes. But relatively few *significant* changes have been made in policies or programs. Many of the needs that were clearly discernible a decade or two ago are still extant; and most of the problems that emanate from the unmet needs are still unresolved. *Moreover, these problems are becoming more acute with each passing month and year.*

The apparent inability of educators and other concerned citizens to effect—and somehow institutionalize—the changes that must be made to meet the needs of an ever-changing society constitutes a major problem. That problem assumes even more serious dimensions when we recognize that *more is known about change and the change process than ever before,* and *more knowledge and expertise relating to planning are available than at any time in our history.* In short, in an era in which there is literally an abundance of knowledge relating to change and the change processes, it becomes difficult to understand why so few meaningful and lasting changes result from the planning that has been accomplished in many state education agencies and local school systems.

Notes

(1) For a detailed description of these and other projects funded under Title V, Section 505, ESEA, see *Emerging State Responsibilities for Education,* Edgar L. Morphet, David L. Jesser, and Arthur P. Ludka, eds. (Denver, Colorado: Improving State Leadership in Education, 1970), pp. 159-168. The reader may wish to also examine the more recent publication: *Planning and Providing for Excellence in Education* (Denver, Colorado: Improving State Leadership in Education, 1971).

(2) Edgar L. Morphet, "Introduction," in *Preparing Educators to Meet Emerging Needs,* Edgar L. Morphet and David L. Jesser, eds. (Denver, Colorado: Designing Education for the Future, March 1969), p. x. Republished by Citation Press, Scholastic Magazines, Inc., New York, New York.

(3) Edgar L. Morphet, "Introduction," in *Planning and Effecting Needed Changes in Education,* Edgar L. Morphet and Charles O. Ryan, eds. (Denver, Colorado: Designing Education for the Future, June 1967), p. vii. Republished by Citation Press, Scholastic Magazines, Inc., New York, New York.

(4) From report on *Planning and Developing an Adequate State Program of Education* by the Study Commission on State Educational Problems, as approved by the National Council of Chief State School Officers. Published in *Education for Victory,* (December 20, 1944), pp. 15-16.

(5) Edgar L. Morphet, Executive Secretary and Editor, *Building a Better Southern Region Through Education* (Tallahassee, Florida: Southern States Work-Conference on Educational Problems, 1945), pp. 57-60.

(6) Progress Reports 1963-67, International Institute for Educational Planning (Paris, France: UNESCO, 1967).

(7) *Designing Education for the Future: Rationale, Procedures and Appraisal,* Edgar L. Morphet and David L. Jesser, eds. (Denver, Colorado: Designing Education for the Future, June 1969), p. 8. The reader may wish to refer to other Designing Education for the Future publications available from Citation Press: *Prospective Changes in Society by 1980* (August 1966); *Implications for*

Education of Prospective Changes in Society (January 1967); *Cooperative Planning for Education in 1980: Objectives, Procedures and Priorities* (January 1968); *Emerging Designs for Education: Program, Organization, Operation and Finance* (May 1968); *Planning for Effective Utilization of Technology in Education* (August 1968).

(8) Edgar L. Morphet, et. al, eds. *Building a Better Southern Region Through Education* (Tallahassee, Florida: Southern States Work-Conference on School Administrative Problems, 1945), p. 44.

(9) Advisory Council on State Departments of Education, *The State of State Departments of Education: Fourth Annual Report,* OE 23050-69 (Washington, D. C.: United States Office of Education, 1969).

(10) See the following case studies:

Arthur P. Ludka, *Planning in the Colorado Department of Education to Facilitate Improvements in Education,* Edgar L. Morphet and David L. Jesser, eds. (Denver, Colorado: Improving State Leadership in Education, 1970), 26 pages.

Lynn P. Cleary, *The Florida Education Improvement Expense Program,* Edgar L. Morphet and Floyd T. Christian, eds. (Denver, Colorado: Improving State Leadership in Education, 1970), 29 pages.

Edward H. Howard and Thomas E. Ogg, *Nevada Master Plan: Providing for Improved Educational Opportunities,* David L. Jesser and Arthur P. Ludka, eds. (Denver, Colorado: Improving State Leadership in Education, 1971), 22 pages.

Keith L. Cruse, *The Evolution of Planning in the Texas Education Agency,* supplement by Laurence D. Haskew, "Implications for Leadership Performance," Edgar L. Morphet and Arthur P. Ludka, eds. (Denver, Colorado: Improving State Leadership in Education, 1970), 23 pages.

Jay J. Campbell and Afton Forsgren, *The Impact of the Designing Education for the Future Project in Utah,* David L. Jesser and Arthur P. Ludka, eds. (Denver, Colorado: Improving State Leadership in Education, 1970), 25 pages.

Charles W. Case, Roger L. Larson, and Peter P. Smith, *Vermont Design for Education,* David L. Jesser and Arthur P. Ludka, eds. (Denver, Colorado: Improving State Leadership in Education, 1971), 29 pages.

George W. Holmes III and William H. Seawell, *Administration by Objectives: A Systematic Approach to Educational Planning in Virginia,* David L. Jesser and Arthur P. Ludka, eds. (Denver, Colorado: Improving State Leadership in Education, 1971), 24 pages.

X

School District Redesign in New York State

Norman D. Kurland and William Webster

The New York State Redesign Project is a comprehensive, systematic process of change involving the participation of a total community in the examination and redefinition of its educational needs and goals. As a change strategy, Redesign deals with the entire system of education and is concerned not only with setting goals and designing programs to facilitate those goals, but is also basically concerned with the developing of an implementation strategy for operationalizing the programs.

While community involvement in achieving more effective and efficient education is a key element in the Redesign process, students and professional personnel also make significant contributions. The State Education Department conceives of its role as being one of guidance, facilitation, encouragement, and stimulation. Viewed from this perspective, Redesign is the development of an education system's capacity and potential to change and adapt continuously to changing needs and objectives.

In order to accomplish this vast and difficult undertaking, Redesign is working in three areas: 1) the initiation of Redesign efforts in four typical communities in the State (the prototypes), 2) the development of capabilities to advance Redesign at the intermediate district level, and 3) the restructuring of the State Education Department to provide the necessary leadership and help on a statewide basis to move toward the new system.

The four prototypes chosen to enable the change process to be studied in depth in different environments were a rural community, a suburban community, a small city, and an inner city school district. Through the development and then analysis of the change efforts in these representative communities, it was believed that programs and processes could be developed and learnings made available to other school districts throughout the State. It was not seen that specific change packages would be developed and reproduced in other districts but rather the process of how a community goes about changing its schools, the problems and pitfalls involved, organizational patterns developed and strategies utilized could be analyzed, and the learnings communicated to the intermediate district level and eventually to the entire State.

Activities in the four initial districts have been generated, analyzed, and passed on to each other and into the intermediate network. One example has been the use of stimulation activities—activities that have as their objectives the mind-stretching of those responsible for educational planning for the future. Therefore, an integral part of Redesign has become an emphasis on the future, with an awareness that decisions made now will affect the lives of people well into the twenty-first century. Further, there is an awareness that, in dealing with the future, so much of what is talked about is conjecture and intuition, since all that we can be sure about the future is that it will be different from the past. However, a determined analysis of trends and projections can be of inestimable help in developing educational plans, making it critical that as people redesign education they take that future into account. Without a solid futures perspective, it is very likely that a redesigned educational program would look very much like the schools of today.

Aware of the vague but certain future, Redesigners see as a central challenge to the Redesign communities the determination of how to create educational arrangements that prepare people to cope with yet unknown futures, while at the same time give them a place and direction in an on-going society. People must have the capacity and the will to help shape that future so that at least it will be a future they have helped to choose. To assist in guidance in this endeavor, Redesign looked to the evolving futures methodology.

It is the recognition of the often nebulous and conjectural nature of futures forecasting that has made long-range planning a keystone of the Redesign effort. It is through long-range planning and the establishment of objectives and futures checkpoints that systems can determine the efficacy and appropriateness of direction of present and planned programs. This continuous analysis is necessary since carrying out future plans often results in something entirely different from what was expected from the plan.

Precisely to avoid falling into the trap of solving only problems of the past and failing to take a comprehensive look at the future, two of the school systems involved in New York State's Redesign Project have become involved in futures programs in order that the change program will be aimed at what things might be rather than emphasizing what things are and what they have been. Each of the systems engaged in futures activities participated in training sessions that dealt with "the kinds of social and technological forces creating the fan of alternative futures for mankind as we approach the year 2000." The principal focus was on the identification of educational goals and educational change strategies needed to increase the likelihood of inventing a more desirable future for mankind. The areas studied were technology, population trends, urbanization, sociological trends, increasing educational demands, ecology, and the need for service-oriented occupations. When some assumptions about the trends were established, both locally, nationally and internationally, beliefs about human nature were considered, including psychological and physiological needs and tendencies of human beings. When the nature of man was related to the possible futures and problems inherent, goals for education began to emerge. The goals included both what the product of the system should be as well as goals for what the system itself should be. (1)

In one of those systems, a small rural district in the western part of the State, eight sessions were held dealing with the future. These sessions dealt with the following topics: 1) basic assumptions about the future, 2) forecasting techniques, 3) long-term trends (two sessions), 4) central human needs in post-industrial society, 5) educational trends, 6) educational requirements for the future, and 7) redesigning education in that community. Sixty people in the community signed up to participate. The number was equally divided with each group of thirty representing students, teachers, board members, and citizens. Reading assignments were given for each session. The format for each session was a short presentation by a futures expert or a film followed by small group discussion. At the close of each evening, the sub-group reporter made a summary report and these reports were compiled, duplicated, and distributed to members the following week.

An interesting development was the discovery on the part of the participants that in this setting they were all learners and, in effect, colleagues, and those who in other settings have been the experts were not expert in this setting as each was beginning to find that he could learn from the other. By focusing on the future the group was able to look beyond the present system and felt able to avoid petty conflict concerning relatively trivial daily events in the school operation. Indirectly, therefore, the future process enabled participants to agree that the present system was inadequate but avoided any carping criticism of the present by dwelling on what it should be.

Obviously, involvement of sixty people in itself is not sufficient to give an entire community a vision of the future. The futures meetings were reported in local newspapers, and participants informally discussed their learnings in a variety of settings. To aid in the dissemination of the futures orientation, a group of twelve people, again representative of all segments of the local system, was brought together over a weekend. As a result of this intensive weekend, initial steps in the writing of a document were taken and the draft turned over to a writing team. Over the ensuing weeks the writing team prepared a document entitled "Education, Human Values, and the Community" for distribution throughout the community and to be followed by discussion in a variety of forums. Changes, alterations, and additions will be built in, and in the meanwhile it will also be distributed throughout the state as an example of the utilization of futures thinking. When the various suggestions are submitted, the writing team will again sit down and prepare a revision of the futures statement. It is, of course, understood that this statement is a vision of the future as seen in 1971-72 and will continue to be under scrutiny, analysis, and alteration each school year in the future.

One group thinking about, talking about, and dreaming for the future, however useful and necessary, is an inadequate response to redesigning a community's educational thinking. The very important nature of the mind-stretching activities of those involved in the futures effort is an important part of Redesign. There must be an awareness, however, that consideration of the future is only one part of a change effort. In order to get a conceptual grasp of the complexity of the problem of change, prototype superintendents, representatives of the State Education Department, and the management consultants have evolved a framework which, in many ways, is a model for conceptualizing the Redesign process. This model looks at the change process as being made up of three areas, each being carried out simultaneously with the other. These areas are planning, program implementation, and management.

The Redesign concept of planning is broader than some may consider the planning process to be. An integral part of the planning phase has become the stimulation activities under the futures rubric. Added to the traditional needs and readiness assessment, these experiences have broadened the concept of needs assessment by encouraging communities to consider needs in terms of the future rather than just the present. This expanded consideration of needs has in turn strongly influenced the processes of objectives and goal setting. Awareness that the consideration of the future and goals and objectives of an educational system should involve more people than just the professional educators has resulted in the intensive effort to involve the wide spectrum of the communities, including students, in the planning phase, and therefore, community recruitment and involvement can be seen as an integral part of the planning effort. The realization that continued recycling of different members of the community in planning over time has meant that the planning process will not be seen as the first phase to be abandoned when programs are implemented but a continuing process.

In the dynamics of the operation of a change effort in an on-going school system, awareness emerged that a planning process cannot endlessly proceed without results. Citizens, teachers and students not directly involved in Redesign, and colleagues in other school systems throughout the state began to demand that evidence of Redesign be presented. The initial reaction was to resist concrete programmatic development but it became apparent that without such development the credibility of Redesign from important segments of the school system's environment could not be gained. Therefore, a program implementation area of the framework was developed.

Three kinds of programs were seen as relating to the Redesign effort. The first program consisted of on-going innovations consistent with the Redesign philosophy, that is, those programs of innovation aimed at changing the school system prior to the Redesign effort that had inherent in them the open, participative elements of Redesign. The second kind of program was designated as immediate and apparent needs programs. In any school system there are needs that immediately become apparent when any substantive analysis is carried on. To prolong the planning process without solving obvious problems would be unfair to youngsters, and, therefore, programs with short-range goals have been initiated as part of Redesigning. The third kind of program was entitled breakthrough programs or those programs that clearly, determinedly, and by design were aimed at making the school system an entirely new system of education and that were the direct product of the Redesign efforts. Each of the three kinds of programs was analyzed to determine if it was consistent with, aimed at, or a part of the total system reform. Crucial to the Redesign program is the determination to avoid piecemeal, patchwork reform and, therefore, each program was reviewed to determine how it meshed with the emerging vision of the future being considered by the school system.

It was a result of the program development activities that the third area of the Redesign framework was brought dramatically to the fore. It became apparent that if the reform activities and the on-going activities were not coordinated, serious disruption of the educational system could result. Awareness of these factors and the need to mesh all activities gave rise to the development of the management area of the framework. As each of the four school systems progressed in the Redesign efforts, management activities were further divided into three areas. First, attention had to be given to the management of the on-going operation of the school system. If adequate and effective attention were not devoted to maintenance of the system, there could not conceivably be anything left to reform. Secondly, effective management of change programs was extremely important if they were to be successful and evaluated as to their reform characteristics. Conceivably, poor management could deprive good plans and good ideas from becoming realities. In addition, it was necessary to compare and evaluate these new programs with the emerging plan to determine their consistency with the vision the system was developing of the future. Thirdly, as new programs were developed and reallocation of resources became a necessity, the smooth meshing of the new programs with the old system was also required.

In summary, as Project Redesign has progressed in New York State, the importance of a comprehensive look at the future has become an integral part of this effort. The importance of a futures view to prevent a replication of tired solutions of the past has become generally accepted. An exciting view of the future, however, has been viewed as being inadequate if not built into the planning process and not expanded to the overall community considering educational change. Planning and future consideration are inextricably bound up with development of new educational programs and in analyzing existing educational programs. Finally, effective and sensitive management at all levels of the total system is necessary if the Redesign effort is to succeed.

Note

(1) The process of the redesign prototypes is emerging. Therefore, more concrete examples are not felt to be appropriate at this time.

Part Four

Applications
of the Futures
Perspective in Teaching

XI

Orienting Hawaii
to the Future:
Multi-Mode Adult Education

James Dator

Unlike any other state in the Union, studying the future has become a legitimate statewide activity in Hawaii. Largely since 1969, when Governor John Burns authorized the creation of an advisory committee to convene a conference on Hawaii 2000, many citizens of the state have been engaged in a great variety of activities with the intent of encouraging and enabling them to gain control over their personal and collective futures.

The Report
of the Hawaii
2000 Chairman

George Chaplin, Editor of the Honolulu *Advertiser,* chairman of the advisory committee, and now chairman of a permanent state commission on Hawaii 2000, summarized the wide variety of futures activities in his report to the Governor and Legislature of December 31, 1971.

The Commission on the Year 2000, created by Act 96 of the 1970 Legislature, is an outgrowth of the Governor's Conference on the Year 2000, established by Executive Order of Governor John A. Burns and held in Honolulu August 5-8, 1970.

Starting early in 1970, a series of interim programs—in the form of future-oriented lectures and panel discussions—was presented to stimulate public interest in the concepts and work of the conference.

Advisory Committee members James Dator and Glenn Paige addressed a joint session of the 1970 State Legislature and they and the Conference Advisory Committee chairman spoke at an annual meeting of the Hawaii State Association of County Officials.

Meanwhile, 10 statewide and 3 Neighbor Island Task Forces with a total membership of some 300 citizens prepared studies to be used as the core of discussions at conference workshops.

The areas studied . . . were: Hawaii's People and Life Style 2000, The Quality of Personal Life 2000, The Natural Environment: Land, Sea and Air 2000, Transportation and Housing 2000, The Economy 2000, Science and Technology 2000, The Arts 2000, Education 2000, Political Decision Making and the Law 2000, Hawaii and the Pacific Community 2000, Hawaii 2000, Maui 2000, Kauai 2000.

The 200 Task Force members and an additional 400 citizens from throughout the state, mostly laymen, were named delegates to the conference. In addition to workshop discussions, they attended plenary sessions featuring: Arthur C. Clarke; Robert Jungk; Yehezkel Dror; Saburo Okita; Charles Williams.

Earlier, at a mini-conference, February 28, 1970, Task Force members heard an address and discussion led by Robert Theobald.

Four prominent futurists attended the August conference as consultant-observers: John McHale, Hahn Been-Lee, Hidetoshi Kato, Raymond Studer.

Alvin Toffler was unable to attend the conference, but in a commentary on film opening the proceedings, he said:

I view this as a pioneer experiment with anticipatory democracy which will be watched closely by other people in London, in Tokyo, in Stockholm and in other centers of the United States . . . I find it particularly appropriate that the first dramatic experiment with anticipatory democracy should take place on an island that lies between Japan and the United States, the two nations whose people, I suspect, are likely to suffer the brunt of future shock before other nations do. . . .

The conference received extensive press coverage in the Honolulu daily papers. Outlines of all Task Force reports were printed, and the conference proceedings themselves were well publicized. As a volunteer project, the Junior Advertising Club of Honolulu had publicized the Hawaii 2000 theme through public service TV and radio and print media advertising.

Following the conference, an Oahu citizens' group, titled "Hawaii's Future," was formed; a future-oriented women's group called "The 70's" was organized; a Big Island 2000 organization was created and a one-day conference held in Hilo with the conference advisory committee chairman as keynote speaker; and a similar conference was conducted on Kauai, with Commission members Dator and Kawakami among the speakers.

Five thousand high school students in the Pacific and Asian Affairs

Council took as their theme for a year's extra-curricular work, "Hawaii 2000: Make it Your World."

The 1971 Legislature enacted legislation creating a Hawaii Research Center for Futures Study at the University of Hawaii.

Other futuristic activities at the University of Hawaii and the East-West Center both preceded and followed the Governor's Conference, including:

- In August 1970, the Second International Conference on the Problems of Modernization in Asia and the Pacific—A Futuristic Perspective, with representatives from 20 Asia-Pacific countries and Hawaii citizens and officials participating.
- From 1969, teaching of more than 30 courses at the University of Hawaii dealing directly with futuristics.
- Four special classes in futuristics for teachers held at the request of the State Department of Education through the College of Continuing Education and Community Service of the University.
- Special innovative grant to explore the development of an interdisciplinary academic program in futures studies at the University.
- Establishment at the Social Science Research Institute of the University of Hawaii a Program in Futures Research.
- More than one hundred community lectures on futuristics by various members of the Commission.

This list indicates the broad nature of the thrust towards the future in Hawaii. Very literally, Hawaii has tried to do everything at once. Rather than starting modestly on one or two fronts and then expanding slowly across the social system, as many arenas as possible have been entered and leading persons from each sector have been encouraged to take responsibility for furthering a futuristic perspective among their own peers.

Why Hawaii?

Without in any way intending to imply that all people have been encouraged to become aware of the future in a different way, nonetheless this broad approach has been gratifyingly successful perhaps partly because of the relative compactness of the State of Hawaii. While the 1.8 million population extends 1,500 miles from the island/county of Kauai to the "Big Island" of Hawaii, about 82% of the population lives on the island of Oahu, where Honolulu is located. The political, economic, intellectual, and social center of the state is thus within easy reach of this 82%.

Honolulu is also a community where many persons are positively oriented to intellectual concerns, and thus could be made more easily aware of futuristics. Activities at the University of Hawaii, for example, frequently merit front page headlines in Honolulu, whereas similar items would be totally ignored in most mainland communities.

Honolulu is also cosmopolitan. Not only is the city ethnically, and hence culturally, mixed, but the hordes of tourists and visitors force diverse change and innovation to be a continuing part of daily life, and prevent any single image of the past from predominating over the future.

Hawaii 2000 chairman George Chaplin refers to Honolulu as a "city-state" having the advantages and disadvantages of such a compact, geographically-isolated, dependent, and yet cosmopolitan community.

Very little direct opposition to the idea of futuristics has been encountered thus far. Futuristic images have clashed—primarily the relative pessimism of the local ecology leaders versus the considerable optimism of the 2000 Commission, or the more short-ranged and violent views of the local radicals versus the more long-ranged and non-violent perspectives of the Commission. There has been apathy and disinterest in some sectors, primarily among lower-class racial minorities very much concerned with the problems of the present. But there has been no group action against the idea of futuristics as such; no argument that there is no need to change or to be concerned about the future; no protestation that the ways of the past are obviously adequate to the challenges from the future.

Sharing Views of the Future in the Community: Exhibits and Interaction

The essence of these activities has been to encourage individual self-determination and control over one's own future. Hence it seems utterly inappropriate to foster a single image of the future, or method for perceiving or achieving it. Our interest so far has been primarily to orient persons to a dimension of time about which they have been relatively ignorant—the future—to help them recognize that they not only can but should turn their attention to this dimension; and to present them with an array of informational sources which will enable them then to go about relating this orientation to their own lives in a way meaningful to themselves—not in uniformity with any particular vision of the persons who happen to be on the Commission.

Concerning participation in exhibits and fairs, the following statement was formulated as to what should be stressed:

It should speak to the people in languages they like and understand. It should "stretch" their minds—not "blow" them. It should certainly inform them.

The visitors to the exhibit should not be told, or shown, or confronted with some more or less pleasing future: they should be encouraged to interact—with each other, with the builders of the exhibit, with the physical objects comprising the exhibit—in considering and themselves designing alternative futures.

Their active consideration of the future in ways they may have never considered it before should be stressed: "We must work together for a better future; we cannot just let it happen. But we must dream undreamed dreams."

The exhibit should be optimistic about the future, about relationships with each other, and to the "natural" environment as well as the man-made environments. The exhibit should not shock, confront, or paralyze the visitors. Rather, it should urge them to positive participation in creating a personally and socially better world.

Such exhibits are seen as integral to teaching and research in futuristics. It is an example of one way in which one can "get out of the ivory tower and among the people," as so many people want. Wherever people are, there we should be, speaking with them about their role in inventing the future—in their homes, their jobs, their clubs, their festivals, using media and messages they understand; urging them to positive action in the design of their own future as well as that of their community. Of course our activities will continue to include lectures, seminars, and the careful, detailed scientific work of the traditionally academic. But there must be continued interaction between the futurist and the members of the community, and the interaction should find expression in as many modes as possible.

Above all, one avoids feeling that he is somehow "bringing the gospel to the heathen." He is not. Views on the future are being shared. Everyone is growing and learning from the interchange. Everyone is becoming more aware of himself, of each other, of shared duty towards the future.

Using Television to "Tune to the Future"

From October 19, 1971 to February 10, 1972, a three-credit course was offered on the local educational television station (KHET-TV) entitled "Tune to the Future." Two hundred twenty-five persons formally enrolled for the course and many more watched regularly throughout the state. Two one-hour shows, almost all of which were taped two weeks in advance, were presented each week (every Tuesday and Thursday at 9 p.m.) for fifteen weeks. The topic outline was as follows:

- Social Change
  Overview of the class
  Our images of the future
  Stability and change; evolution and adaptation

The experience of social change—before and after the agricultural
   revolution
The experience of social change—the industrial revolution and
   mass-produced man
Mass-produced diseases of the present—alienation, overpopulation, pollution, exhaustion of resources, overkill.
Some probable alternative futures

- Technologies that are shaping the future
How technology shapes the future
Computers, automation and cybernation
Artificial intelligence
New sources of food, fuels, and materials
Transportation and communication for the future
Outer space and under the seas
The biological revolution—toward utopian motherhood
The biological revolution—is death just a curable disease?
The biological revolution—some of my best friends are cyborgs

- Elements for determining the future
The need for creativity and imagination
New ideas of beauty
Christianity and pollution—the sound of one hand coughing
Science and the social science
Special live show with John McHale and Chief Abedo, head of
   UNITAR

- Some possible value and institutional changes in the future
Human values and human valuing—from conformity to choice
Learning to become—changing modes of education
Families in transition
Changing sex and age roles—you be the mommie and I'll be the
   daddy this time
Social decision making and conflict resolution—new modes of
   government
Techniques of social prediction and design
Design of futures exercise (I and II)
Wrap up

One-half of every fourth show (that is, thirty minutes out of every
four hours) was a live question-and-answer session wherein viewers
were encouraged to phone in their questions for direct answers on the
show. In addition, four "community meetings" for the class members
were held in different places in Oahu, and one each on Maui and
Hawaii. These meetings were held on an evening of one of the regular
telecasts and commenced about one hour before the program began
with questions about the course in general. For the next hour, that
evening's show was watched, and specific questions answered for
about a half hour more.

Each program included mixes of the following components:

- Interviews with experts. Video-taped or sound-sinc filmed interviews or monologues.
- Survey-interviews with "common people" getting their off-the-cuff reaction to specific questions about the future. Audio tape and 35 mm slides.
- Aiglatson (that's "nostalgia" spelled backwards). One-liners and quotations about the future. Video-taped in the studio.
- Future flashes (news flashes from the future). Video-taped in the studio.
- Excerpts from films, or sometimes entire existing motion pictures relating to the future.
- Specially filmed or video-taped skits or demonstrations.
- Video-taped slide presentations with narration and music.
- Dator lecturing on camera in the TV studio or filmed on location.

Because television presented us with a different medium that should be utilized differently, "Laugh-In" was taken as a model. A strictly linear mode of communication was avoided, and by taping various segments during the week and putting them together into a final show, the "theme in discontinuity" was maintained. Both from the students' own evaluations and our impressions, the course seemed rather successful in reaching the goals set out above—generally speaking, it seems to have challenged without shocking and instructed without boring.

Goals of the Commission on Hawaii 2000

Self-consciously futuristic activities will probably continue and proliferate. The State of Hawaii, through the State Research Center for Futures Studies and the Program for Futures Research in the Social Science Research Institute of the University of Hawaii, has indicated its desire to further basic and applied research into the future. The Futures Studies Program of the University, in conjunction with the College of Continuing Education, seeks to bring together a growing variety of disciplinary courses on the future, and to encourage their expansion on the elementary and secondary school level (there are already such classes in existence). But the main work on adult education towards the future remains that of the State Commission on Hawaii 2000 which has set forth a very ambitious program designed to bring a futures orientation into the society generally. The goals of the Commission as reported to the Governor and Legislature in 1971 read as follows:

1. To create, sustain and intensify an awareness among Hawaii's people that our future may be and is being shaped in several different ways, and how this may occur and is now occurring; and

2. (a) To promote and maintain the active participation and involvement of Hawaii's people in a statewide effort to depict and assess political, economic, social, cultural and environmental goals for Hawaii;

   (b) To devise and recommend legislative, administrative, and citizen action to accomplish these goals.

   (c) To assess, evaluate and review periodically these goals and the action being undertaken to accomplish them; and

3. To promote, assist and coordinate programs, activities and plans of individuals and organizations, whether public or private, directly concerned with the future of Hawaii.

It is the hope that "futuristics" in Hawaii and elsewhere will eventually fade away into the fabric of society. It is, in the author's opinion, an *orientation,* not a methodology and certainly not a philosophy—the word "futuristics," is used instead of "futurology" or "futurism" for that reason. Once one is oriented, he can simply go in the direction he wishes.

XII

Futurizing a Multiversity: The University of Minnesota Experience

Arthur Harkins
and Richard Woods

The Office for Applied Social Science and the Future, within the University of Minnesota's Center for Urban and Regional Affairs, was created on July 1, 1971. It primarily exists to add to the growth of organizations focusing upon alternative futures within the central part of the United States. Specifically, the Office is concerned with the development of graduate and undergraduate courses on alternative futures, and with the packaging of these courses into degree programs. The Office is concerned with the kinds of research and development programs which will fit campus interests, and which also will contribute to the formation of courses and programs on alternative futures. Finally, the Office is concerned with the interface between campus and community, specifically with large corporations reevaluating their roles in American society. We consider among our most important past activities the establishment of six undergraduate and graduate courses on alternative futures at the University of Minnesota; the establishment of the Office itself; and the sharpening of our own role definitions through these activities and through the working frameworks established by grants with outside agencies.

Our most interesting projects in 1972, besides establishing further undergraduate and graduate programs in alternative futures, are: contract work on the wide-band new town community information system at Jonathan, Minnesota; contract work with the United States Army Corps of Engineers on alternative future uses of water resources; and a contract with the Northern States Power

Corporation in an extensive, sophisticated management training adult education program on alternative futures for a select population of NSP personnel.

Academic Course Development

Since the primary focus of the Office is to gather, evaluate and disseminate information concerning alternative human futures, curriculum and degree development on the campus of the University of Minnesota have been a major part of its initial efforts. The bulk of this curriculum development has taken place in three sectors of the University: Social Science, Education, and the Office of Special Learning Opportunities (home of the new undergraduate Future Studies major). In Education, some sections of the course "School and Society" are being "retooled" to emphasize alternative social possibilities with emphasis upon the role and status of future education systems. "Social Science and Systems Perspectives" is set up to provide a basic introduction to systems analysis and social science methodologies and important theories, both concerned with education. A non-prerequisite sequence of courses has been set up emphasizing education-related social change actualities and possibilities in different "time frames" (about one decade, one to three decades, and three decades and beyond, respectively. Two intercultural education courses taught by Harkins have been restructured to emphasize future possibilities of poor and non-white people in the United States, paying special attention to the crucial role of educational systems. The Social Science Program, "Societies of the Future" has been set up and taught several times by Office staff. This course emphasizes the growing science of futurology, and requires fairly demanding reading in a growing body of literature. Three seminars in "Alternative Futures" have been instituted, and have involved the services of approximately thirty faculty and industrial executives during 1971-1972. It is anticipated that these three seminars will have four sections each quarter during 1972-1973, and will bring an additional 145 faculty, industry officers, legislators and regents together to discuss alternative futures. In addition to these courses and seminars, the staff of the Office for Applied Social Science and the Future, working closely with faculty members from several departments, has assisted in the development of:

- A 14-credit "package" future education course for College of Education seniors. This "package" stretches over an entire academic year, and involves two departments within the College of Education. The primary focus of the course is to develop a futures curriculum emphasis in an inner city Minneapolis junior high school.
- A pair of "semi-automated" courses for Future Studies majors in Liberal Arts. These two courses will be concerned with the cultural

history of futurology (including much emphasis upon anthropological literature), as well as emphasizing futures methodologies.

- A futures tape archive in the University of Minnesota language laboratory. The tapes will be available to all students, both undergraduate and graduate, who are interested in pursuing future studies. Tapes are being acquired for this purpose in 1972.

Liberal Arts Major
in Future Studies

On January 1, 1972, the College of Liberal Arts at the University of Minnesota established a major in Future Studies through its Office of Special Learning Opportunities (OSLO). During the Summer of 1971, personnel of OSLO began a survey of course catalogs to determine roughly what courses might be applicable to a proposed Future Studies major. After these courses were isolated, faculty were interviewed by telephone during the Fall quarter of 1971 and asked whether these or other courses would be suitable to a proposed Future Studies major. The result of this effort was the formulation of a draft brochure on Future Studies including many courses directly and indirectly concerned with the examination of alternative futures. (1) Donald Myrvik, director of OSLO, later divided the many identified courses into three tracks: social sciences; natural sciences; and the humanities and arts. Within each of these areas, a half dozen or more faculty were identified who agreed to become counselors to Future Studies majors and to give preference to these majors in the case of requests for reading courses or special academic credit experience. Also located were over a dozen faculty outside the College of Liberal Arts who were willing to counsel and provide special academic help to Future Studies majors.

Will Minnesota Develop
a Graduate Futures Studies Capability?

Early in 1972, staff members of the Office for Applied Social Science and the Future, working with many interested faculty at the University of Minnesota, were investigating the possibility of a graduate degree program in Future Studies, to be offered by some department or program within the University structure. While the undergraduate major in Future Studies required very little initiation funding (the great bulk of courses were offered as a matter of routine by the various departments involved), the graduate Future Studies Program will require some new funding for "borrowed" faculty from other departments. These "borrowed" faculty would not be new in the sense of new faculty holding added positions, but would be "bought" for a portion of their time from their own departments in order to offer graduate futures seminars, courses and counseling services.

Graduate Future Studies immediately suggests quality controls—strict ones. Professor H. Wentworth Eldredge, a Dartmouth sociologist, is completing a new critique of largely undergraduate future courses in selected colleges and universities. While the survey was begun prior to the development of Future Studies courses at Minnesota, Eldredge earlier warned against intellectually faulty work in the area: (2)

1) *Shallow intellectual roots.* Persons conducting futures courses showed little awareness of mankind's historical and prehistorical struggles.

2) *Absence of Social Change theory.* Little was noted in the way of adequate treatment of social change theory, with the exception of a few sociologists' courses.

3) *Epistemological Problems.* It was concluded from all the courses on which data were available that the epistemological underpinnings for futures courses were very poorly developed.

4) *Faulty or Incomplete Teaching Methods.* Eldredge obviously felt uneasy over "groovy" teaching methods by "with it" teachers for "hip" students.

These criticisms provide useful warning signals to anyone planning graduate courses or degree programs in Future Studies. But since inveighing against sin is insufficient by itself, what major ingredients might a viable Future Studies graduate program offer? Keeping in mind Eldredge's warnings, let us offer one scenario broadly suggestive of program content and style.

The program offers the opportunity for graduate students to inquire, through interdisciplinary analysis, into problems of social specialization and generalization with the time frame of thirty years and more into the future. Projections and analyses of long-range social and technological trends related to American culture are made. Students are asked to read certain basic materials on long-range trends in the development of American and world society. Historical and anthropological material are especially useful in this regard.

Students are asked to inquire into a variety of institutional futures related to American society. They are asked to read and hypothesize about the development of the economy, about the future of democracy, the future of international conflicts, man's genetic and ecological future, race relations, the future of morals and social beliefs, etc. A constant focus of the program is the development of alternative social futures as understood through multi-institutional analysis. Students are asked to develop models for societies of the future and then to work these models "backward" into the present in order to test their "fit" and to gain insights into actual development prospects. Students also are asked to investigate the accuracy of these predictions and some means by which the predictions might be altered.

The entire program stresses the application of interdisciplinary analysis to the problems of specialization and generalization of human understanding, with emphasis upon the future of formal and informal social systems. The program provides students with opportunities to investigate, discuss, debate and evaluate many aspects of the anticipated impacts of long-range social trends (such as computer controlled education systems, political, economic, social and moral structural changes, etc.). Instruction stresses the interaction of the social sciences, business, humanities and arts with basic facets of long-range social development. A spirit of vigorous and disciplined inquiry is promoted, with the intent that all of the long-range alternatives pertaining to human societies remain open to examination, and with assurances that each alternative is given a fair hearing. Graduate students in the Future Studies Program routinely approach their work in three time frames—not simply a "futures" one.

To help them deal effectively with these and many other questions, graduate students in the Future Studies Program are provided with ample counseling, in addition to department courses and interdisciplinary seminars. The courses, counseling and seminars in each student's total program of study are regarded as crucial for providing an opportunity to compare and synthesize many important intellectual experiences; for this reason, they are thorough and demanding.

In all of this work, Future Studies Program faculty and graduate students are assisted by visits from knowledgeable and even renowned off-campus persons; two-way amplified telephone lectures and discussions bring distant scholars and practitioners into the classroom; a tape bank of futures materials is available in the language laboratory; video tapes from the World Future Society are on call at the Office for Applied Social Science and the Future; certain "automated" courses are available with printed lectures and other materials and services, all routinely updated.

Whether or not the University of Minnesota can mount a graduate program in Future Studies within its structure was unknown to us early in 1972. The planning which already has gone into a Future Studies graduate program can, however, be shifted to improving the Future Studies undergraduate major in Liberal Arts. Early in 1972 funds were being sought to support a Future Studies graduate degree program should the decision be made to implement one.

Futurizing a Multiversity:
Some Strategic Considerations

Conventional planning and futures planning are often indistinguishable because of normative constraints. At best, conventional planning and futures planning are distinguished by fundamental epistemological differences. These differences are expressed most often in the greater provision to futures planners of alternatives that are *really* alternatives and not simply variations around largely inflexible "givens." The best approach to futurizing a university or college suggests an open planning process, involving all interested or potentially interested persons and groups. The open process also communicates all planning information, strategies, tactics, etc., to the *outside* community for additional feedback. Choice of the mix between professional futurists and others is mediated by the conditions of the various states of the art involved, the nature of the world views of those involved, the constraints of particular situations, and the feedback of potentially affected persons inside or outside the college or university. Approaching the future on an entirely *ad hoc* basis, an entirely normative basis, or an entirely extrapolative basis seems inadequate in each case.

The Office of Applied Social Science and the Future thinks of "power" as the development, maintenance, and utilization of wide-ranging *functional* alternatives within any particular set of constraints. A key element in this definition of power becomes the actual ability to exercise flexibilities that are intimately related to the range of available armchair alternatives. In order to prevent this process from becoming uncontrolled, ingrown, or potentially harmful to the university or college community, personnel of this Office feel that completely open feedback of collegiate futures planning inside and outside the institution is fundamentally necessary. Thus, any internal or external interest may attempt to constrain any practical exercise by collegiate futurists of "power" as we have defined it here. Open planning and feedback processes will, we believe, constrain the over-zealous, particularly where "empire building" or bureaucratic nucleation are involved.

Futurizing a Multiversity:
Some Tactical Considerations

Specifically, we suggest the following grassroots approaches for futures activists within higher education institutions:

1) Show people *The Futurist*. Many have not seen it before, and there are few who are not delighted with it after a few moments of examination. Help them subscribe before other matters capture their attention. (3)

2) Institutional memberships in the World Future Society are invaluable, practically and symbolically. In Minnesota, the Twin Cities alone has at least a half dozen institutional memberships in the World Future Society, and more are on the way. The Office for Applied Social Science and the Future has been an Institutional Member for more than one year, and it is expected that the University of Minnesota Board of Regents and the University of Minnesota Foreign Student Association will become members in February or March, 1972.

3) Avoid talk of hiring new faculty. With the higher education budgetary pessimism so prevalent in 1972, it is far better to futurize existing faculty and to discover futurized faculty within the ranks. This enables the creation of an "invisible college" of future oriented faculty, who may begin discussions as to how their mutual interests might be expressed.

4) Interdisciplinary seminars on alternative futures are invaluable for bringing together diverse community and faculty interests. The University of Minnesota began with three such seminars in 1971-72; it expects to have between nine and twelve such seminars in 1972-73.

5) Keep the academic quality of futures courses and seminars above reproach. Nothing, as H. Wentworth Eldredge has noted, is more devastating to the serious study of alternative futures than "blue sky" courses and shallow, undisciplined academic "activity." In this regard, a reading of the Eldredge article cited in this chapter may be helpful.

6) Involve off-campus persons with reputations for vigorous, competent futurist activities. By this, we mean industry officers, legislators, regents, trustees, politicians, bureaucrats, consultant professionals, community leaders and others whose activities fall within a very broad definition of "futurist." Our operational definition of a futurist is simple and inclusive: a competent person who looks ahead to alternative futures of possible importance to human welfare. Such persons will comprise 50 per cent of all "faculty" giving papers within the University of Minnesota seminars on alternative futures in 1972-73.

7) Give papers at national professional society meetings. In the last year and four months, personnel from the Office for Applied Social Sciences of the Future have read papers at an American Anthropological Association symposium on cultural futures, and will read papers at five more major national social science meetings within the next fourteen months. Properly handled, these activities can go a long way towards acquainting faculty all over the country with futures emphases developing within particular disciplines.

8) Exercise public caution using the label, "futurist." Most "futurists" are still disciplinarians in some major degree. This

point may seem trivial, but we have seen many occasions where cultish labeling has resulted in much less than the planned-for reactions.

Some Concluding Acknowledgments

Virtually none of the futures courses and seminars at the University of Minnesota would be possible without the donation of time and other resources by faculty from several area colleges and universities. Industry officers also have been invaluable as paper-giving seminar "faculty" and as very useful sources of practical advice. Hundreds of students have improved our courses and seminars through written and verbal critiques, and radio listeners have added to this process through their letter and telephone responses to broadcast seminars. Further developments, particularly in the current years of fiscal austerity, will probably depend upon a continued refinement of the "open door" approach to academic futures courses, seminars, and degree programs. Industry officers, legislators, and community intellectuals will almost certainly assist faculty and students immensely in the coming years of intellectual expansion signalled by the serious study of alternative human futures.

Notes

(1) An updated version of the futures studies brochure (prepared by Donald Myrvik) is available from the Office for Applied Social Science and the Future, 720 Washington Ave. S.E., University of Minnesota, Minneapolis, Minn. 55455.

(2) H. Wentworth Eldredge, "Education for Futurism in the United States: An Ongoing Survey and Critical Analysis," *Technological Forecasting and Social Change,* 2 (1970), pp. 133-148. For a briefer version, see "Education in Futurism in North America," *The Futurist,* IV:5, (Dec. 1970), pp. 193-196. For further information on the 1972 survey, write H. Wentworth Eldredge, Dept. of Sociology, Dartmouth College, Hanover, N. H. 03755.

(3) Mailing address: World Future Society, P. O. Box 19285, Twentieth Street Station, Washington, D. C. 20036. Membership in WFS costs $7.50 annually and includes the bi-monthly magazine.

XIII

Problems and Prospects
for Educational Futuristics

Billy Rojas

Futuristics began as a subspecialty within military science. In recent years the field—which is actually an attitude among professionals in a wide range of disciplines—has moved toward becoming an establishment science. The methods of economic forecasters, political pollsters and demographers coexist with the techniques employed by technological forecasters; all of which is obviously relevant to traditional long-range planning. Thus, while few business firms or government agencies know how to utilize "futures research" as well as General Electric or the Institute of Life Insurance, even fewer organizations now fail to perceive the need for it. And unlike the ecology movement futuristics has been, to date, an institutional phenomenon. The people who have "turned on" to empirical futuristics have been above ground, organization men. Few things demonstrated this quite so well as the population that attended the First General Assembly of the World Future Society in Washington, D. C., during May of 1971. Conspicuous by their absence were blacks, Chicanos, Puerto Ricans, Indians or members of other racial minorities. Women were under-represented. Also hard to find were the scores of younger, long-hair students who might have been expected. The shift of interest toward serious speculation about the future has so far been a shift of interest on the part of middle aged males who hold leadership positions of the middle management type. It has been a development within the establishment.

The Growth of Futures Courses

Futuristics also is quickly becoming an academically respectable discipline, field, viewpoint (circle one). The growth of futuristics courses in colleges and universities has been exponential. In 1968 about sixteen courses that could be classified as future studies were being offered at various schools in the United States and Canada. This figure had jumped to seventy (give or take some) at the start of the 1970 academic year. Throughout 1971 results of an ongoing survey conducted by the author and H. Wentworth Eldridge at Dartmouth indicated that what might be termed a "takeoff point" had been reached. In early 1972 the number exceeded 300 and showed no signs of a diminished rate of progress. Unfortunately a comprehensive survey of futures work in elementary and secondary classrooms does not seem to have been attempted so far. But straws are in the wind here, too: dozens of them, perhaps hundreds. (1) Mentioning these dimensions of the futures movement within the educational establishment, then, serves to indicate the reality of that phenomenon. Futuristics is not a hypothetical hand about to write on the wall; teachers, administrators and students are already responding to a visible message.

Demand for academic futures experiences can only be expected to increase during the next year, if not longer, until possibly the majority of the nation's schools become involved. Interest is being generated by the appearance of a considerable literature advertising the educational merits of one or another futuristics approach to learning. And one book, Alvin Toffler's *Future Shock,* is obviously stimulating an academic tidal wave of its own. Jerome Agel's *Teacher's Guide to Future Shock* had reached 43,000 teachers within little more than a month of its publication. Students can be expected to provide impetus of their own. Since late 1971 the paperback edition of the Toffler opus, as reported in the *Chronicle of Higher Education,* has been at the top of the list of campus bookstore purchases. Presumably those books are being read and, once this happens, people can then articulate their distinctly modern malaise: future starvation. "When do we eat?" then becomes a pressing question.

Doubtless the majority of academic futurists today could be considered traditional in their classroom approach. In college courses surveyed, most learning relied upon well tried methods. Lectures, discussions, tests and writing assignments predominated. Yet to note the present configuration of the field is hardly adequate. In futuristics the exceptions are not only more interesting but they also may be highly indicative of things to come. It might even be argued that exceptions within the futures movement are ultimately normative. For what is happening is that a number of young graduates with an innovative outlook have been attracted to futuristics during the past few years and, at the same time, older teachers have perceptibly changed their pedagogy as a result of the new parameters implicit in any forward-looking time orientation. Maintaining an historical methodology, one discovers while pursuing futures teaching or research, is the wrong response to the problems one is trying to cope with.

Any analysis of the futures movement within American schools needs to take account of the fact that futuristics causes secondary effects of its own. Thinking about the future means thinking in terms of alternatives, for there is no one tomorrow waiting to be "predicted" by professional forecasters. The future, admitting obvious constraints such as budgetary commitments, available technology, and geography, is still radically open. The shape of the future can be altered by human intervention. Whether those who carry out the shaping are voters, consumers, engineers or faculty members is of concern, surely, but the discovery by a teacher that initiatives have foreseeable consequences alters one's perceptual horizons. In some cases the results are educationally radical. Futuristics is in the establishment; it remains to be seen if it can possibly remain *of* the establishment.

Some New Teaching Styles

Some impressive departures from traditional teaching styles can be reported here. As examples one can cite the work of Dennis Livingston while he was at Case Western Reserve, Al Record of Rutgers, and Jose Villegas now at Columbia. Villegas conducted a series of long duration games during 1969-1971. These classroom games took a variety of forms: cards were sometimes used, simulated elections were employed at times, investing influence points was another possibility. Research was ordinarily required of Villegas' students between rounds of those games. In *Ghetto 84,* a city simulation game, each of eight weeks of a term represented a 2 year period of real time ending in 1984. Students became community spokesmen and various groups within the class represented black people, affluent whites, working class whites, etc. Each group was expected to make plausible decisions about how resources would be allocated—what part of available funds should be invested in housing or business ventures. A balance sheet showing cumulative changes in each neighborhood was maintained and, as the climax of each class meeting, the effects of change were manifest during simulated elections for city government.

In Record's classes at the Livingston College branch of Rutgers students engage in encounter-type meetings. The purpose of these sessions (which are held during the first weeks of the term and then discontinued) is to create a community from the aggregation of students enrolled in the course. Record structures these sessions, however, so that participants, including himself, are able to focus upon the problems of learning. Individual identity as a student, after all, means that the way in which one can come to know something is crucial. Rather than ignoring the issues of learning difficulties and individual differences, Record attempts to turn them into an academic asset. Then students can approach questions such as "what is futuristics?" in its education dimensions. Further, on the assumption that learning how to deal with the 21st century is inhibited by traditional teaching styles, Record's students play the "Totalitarian Classroom Game;" the outcome is that the class and its teacher drop stereotypes and try to create new learning roles. Record is a senior learner, group facilitator and class participant rather than an instructor.

Dennis Livingston, it can be said, has also developed another new teaching role: the professor as fellow traveler. In 1970 Livingston created a course in a completely new specialty, spatial futuristics. "California as Wave of the Future," held during a one-month January term, consisted of a three and one half week expedition from Cleveland, Ohio to the west coast. This journey was preceded by several more-or-less ordinary class meetings during which discussions of several books reflecting upon California's future and its qualities as a barometer for the rest of the United States were held. After disembarking at the airport the class visited various institutions and communities in the Golden State that quite possibly anticipated by several years the character of different populations throughout America.

Futurists, as can be seen, are also free from traditional content restraints. And even when methodological departures are not so great as those just described, the learning problems posed are sometimes novel indeed. James Duran teaches a course at Canisius College that treats history as it has yet to be treated elsewhere. Duran studies the view of the future that historical personages have entertained. Then he probes the record to determine how various types of future perspectives influenced the decisions of Catherine the Great, Napoleon or Mussolini. Other content areas are in evidence, as well, among futurists. Ronald Abler teaches a class in "The Geography of the Future" at Pennsylvania State. Thomas D. Harblin teaches a course dealing with families in the future at Colorado State. One trend has also developed that is new to liberal arts, the single population class. Apparently the first example of this was Dennis Little and Raul De Brigard's course at Wesleyan in 1970 entitled "The Future of Middletown." Students studied the governmental structure of this Connecticut community, analyzed the sociology of the town and made specific predictions about its future. These forecasts were the types of statement of some value to city planners. The most recent example of this kind is one recently concluded by the author called "The Future of Appalachia."

Such departures are not limited to the college level.

One intriguing venture was carried out by Patricia Burke at Mark's Meadow Elementary School in Amherst, Massachusetts. Biologists and physicians have brought us to the place where genetic engineering—the deliberate redesign of one's own body—is a distinct possibility. In fact, for specialized purposes (plastic surgery, prostheses) one can see indications of what the impact of true genetic manipulation could be. Patricia Burke decided to move one step further. Working with felt she cut out some 80 body parts—arms, legs, torsos, etc.—that could be placed on a flannel board. These parts catered to a wide variety of physiological tastes. Besides human limbs of various colors and proportions children could select animal body parts such as wings. Or they could chose to become cyborgs by imcorporating vacuum hoses, computers, wheels or other technological improvements into their persons. Children working in pairs at the flannel board could determine, by putting together some combination of body parts, what kind of appearance they desired for themselves: their body for the year 2000. This exercise in imagination for students, however, was also an opportunity for Patricia Burke to find out some facts about her pupils. What sort of attitude do they have toward their present bodies? What kind of value system underlies the selection of body components they make? The future, it is plain, can be a resource for learning as well as subject matter.

Some Problems in Acceptance

In all of this, however, are buried some problems. Some difficulties arise, from the newness of the field. With what does one follow up the future body activity? What are legitimate objectives for California as Wave of the Future? Other problems are more fundamental. People may be enthusiastic about studying alternative futures but the values and presuppositions inherent in American culture mitigate against prognostication. Students as well as their teachers often carry three biases with them, at least during their initial encounter with futuristics, that work against obtaining sophistication in dealing with futures themes. A cliche' is one of these obstacles. Americans have been guarded against even a minimal degree of speculative *savoir faire* by the slogan, "you can't know the future." I can think of no single, powerful source for this wisdom but it doesn't take long to hear it from a professor's lips or to read it in a journal. The authority behind the constant iteration of the idea not only serves to validate it but also seems to cast aspersions on quite another activity altogether, namely, learning how to anticipate change. True enough, philosophies have been conceived which attempt to do just this but—and here is the second point—each has become identified with some political axe-to-grind. Most obvious is the case of Karl Marx. It was not too many years ago when learning anything from Marx, such as the desirability of looking at modifications in the relationships between social classes, was disreputable because he wrote the Old Testament of communism. Finally, one should mention the anti-planning attitude of many Americans. This legacy of Adam Smith, however questionable it is to professional economists, is still very much alive in the minds of non-professionals. It is better to let the invisible hand guide events, or to let fate, God, or luck, do the job than deliberately to draft working drawings that organize one's time. There is no doubt that these constraints have far less strength than they did a generation ago but it is also true that they still operate. Futuristics cannot be generally successful unless it replaces such myths in the public mind with myths that generate more fruitful attitudes.

Forecasting Techniques in the Classroom

More pertinent than this, however, is the identification of futuristics in the public mind with the establishment. In other words futuristics, like pharmacy or the law, may be perceived as inaccessible. What can ultimately overcome this feeling is popularization of empirical forecasting methods so that their utility can be recognized. One is left with the impression that when all is said and done futuristics is basically an *art*. Classroom teachers need to discover how to employ forecasting methods; even considerable pedagogical experimentation cannot compensate for the absence of these methods to facilitate the process of learning.

Two forecasting techniques are especially appropriate for futures research courses or units elsewhere within the curriculum: the creative problem solving system known as brainstorming and Delphi surveys. Both methods have been used in a number of college courses and Howard Peelle, also working at Mark's Meadow Elementary School, has devised a computer mediated Delphi exercise in which children become "experts" and forecast future events. This list can probably be expanded, however.

Experiments with students at Alice Lloyd College have demonstrated that even sophisticated forecasting methods can be redesigned for classroom use. Cross-impact prognoses can be obtained, for instance, by a very simple expedient. A card containing a sentence that describes a possible future event is easy to prepare. "1975: Sex-selector pill becomes available on the United States market; prospective parents can choose the sex of their children." At that point several options are open to the teacher. The card can simply be circulated from student to student (if the class is reasonably small) each one adding, in turn, a consequence that might follow from the supposed event. The object in this would be unpretentious, to create a condition requiring students to take a serious look at the future. The possible impact of an event upon subsequent history as conjectured by one's students may not be the model of logical causality or inductive reasoning but their attention has been directed forward in time, they will have considered a serious problem and speculated about its ramifications.

The very simplicity of this device permits adaptation for a variety of purposes. Sex related differences of opinion can be elicited and then discussed. All that is needed is to write the same future event on two cards, one of which is then circulated only among men, the other only among women. Another version of this exercise consists of dividing a class into small groups each with a role to play, for example, American business, state government, the religious establishment, counter-culture. One event can then serve to stimulate discussion about the diversity of consequences that can result from a single contingency. It is a short step from such exercises to the construction of cross-impact matrices and then into considerations of the method itself.

Scenarios can be created in classrooms with as little difficulty as cross-impact consequences. And one modification that involves literary considerations may hold interest for readers. During a course devoted to the subject of space exploration, students were presented with the first paragraph of a science fiction story set in the future. Reference was made to several themes pertinent to astronomic theory then being studied in the class. The students, one after another, developed the story by contributing a new paragraph of their own to it. The final version of the adventure could then be evaluated by the class along several dimensions: coherency, credibility, content, etc. Also possible would be a classroom exercise in which each student individually completed the story so that, at the end of an hour, a score of science fiction sagas each starting from the same point would be available. Certainly students would be interested in what their classmates had written and why the same background information suggested different conclusions. All of this also, and not incidentally, says much about the problems of futuristics.

After a suitable range of forecasting methods have been tried in class, competency can be tested by the teacher. The history of some country—Belgium, Burma, Brazil—for a limited time period, say 1900 until 1945, can be written and distributed to students. They are then asked to review the history before them and use forecasting methods to predict the "future" of the nation in question, for example, 1946-1972. Instant feedback. Similarly, short-range events that actually lie in the future can be utilized in this same fashion. What will be the outcome on the next election day?

Summary

All of which is a far cry from military science or, for that matter, management science. But then, the contention of this paper is that futuristics is volatile. One should not expect it to remain unchanged as it moves between different environments and different individuals. One should expect rather dramatic transformations in the style of speculating when the youth movement takes up futuristics in a committed way, for example. One might also expect to see new organizational styles emerge from the creation of futuristic educational groups if this contention is correct. In what ways will new futures centers, schools, and groups be different than non-futures bodies? An answer to that question is premature at present but if futuristics does have sufficient power to generate academic change, the question will be answered affirmatively.

Note

(1) See following essay by James Oswald.

The Future
as a School Subject

James M. Oswald

Study of the future is an appropriate subject-methodology for schools whose students are preparing for adult lives in the society we are creating. Anything less than educating for the future is indefensible, anti-educational. Yet schools, even the best of them, rarely place primary emphasis upon preparing for and creating the future. This tragedy, the tragedy of backward looking curriculums, is being discussed more and more.

The concern of this paper is an overview of what is happening in elementary and secondary schools as regards the future and the "futurization of knowledge." (1) Of first importance is clarifying the meaning of terminology. By "the future" and "futures" we mean concern with *alternative futures,* both desirable and undesirable. There are many possible futures. We can create any of several, and our creating of the future can be either a conscious, semi-conscious, or unconscious process by which desires, expectations, and realities are intermixed through time to produce change. We also mean to communicate, in using the terms "future" and "futures," that neither we or anyone else know exactly what the future will be like. We are interested in forecasting the future and in designing the future. We are interested in encouraging and enabling students to do likewise. But this futurizing must be done modestly for there are uncontrollable realities which we cannot change. And there are horrible possible futures which, while interesting and worthwhile to study, ought to be resisted before they develop. Hence, our use of futurism is not blind. It is not hopeful escapism. It is not a denial of reality. It is optimistic, but only moderately so. This futurism, which seems appropriate for school students to be aware of and participate in, is not predetermined. It is developing, as the following paragraphs will indicate.

An opportunity for futures courses is created by the contemporary shift of educational programs away from traditional emphasis on memorization and toward an emphasis on inquiry. Of the subjects open to inquiry—the past, present, and future—are examples of broad categories arranged in the order they have been considered. Inquiry leads easily from concern with where did we come from to a concern with who we are and where we are going. And it presents a danger. For inquiry can decay into mysticism when inquirers lack perspective and expertise. Unwarranted cynicism or optimism can evolve from frivolous inquiry. As Festinger pointed out in *When Prophecy Fails* (1956), (2) lack of knowledge and the failure of predictions to materialize can deepen the convictions of true believers. It is important that the rational, scientific, and aesthetic qualities of futurism be stressed in school programs, and that irrational, anti-scientific, mystical "Futurology" be studied for understanding, but not implemented. Sanity and reasonableness can be protected and developed through serious inquiry into alternative futures. Along the way, it is important to keep the values of tentativeness and suspended judgment as a balance for forecasts of the future.

Some Examples of Who Is Doing What

A limited number of schools have planned or offered futures courses. A greater but undetermined number have probably futurized some aspect of their traditional courses in language arts, mathematics, science, and social studies. For every teacher of "Alternative Futures" there are likely to be at least a dozen who have incorporated science fiction or forecasting, or scenario writing into their courses.

The following examples suggest the variety of developments in future study:

- The Stanford University School of Education formed a task force which spent a year studying alternative futures for their own institution and its programs. This group considered probable future changes in schools and society and is reorganizing its efforts to prepare educators for the future.
- The Mattapoissett, Massachusetts Central Schools planned an elective futures course for high school students based on a syllabus developed by a teacher committee led by a young social studies supervisor, Philip Devaux.
- John Weil designed and teaches a "Global Prospects" course at Harwood High School in Moretown, Vermont.

- Jane Gaughan, of the Central Junior High School in Quincy, Massachusetts, integrated an alternative futures theme into the seventh and eighth grade language arts classes which she teaches.
- Two Minneapolis, Minnesota teachers, Tom Bender and Scott Helmes, initiated a futuristic summer school program. Their students built model cities, role played "another person," and thought about the future.
- Lloyd Kehu teaches a futuristic course in Los Gatos, California, in the Pacific Domes School.
- Jon Dieges works with students who are designing cities of the future in Berkeley's Willard Junior High School and Martin Luther King Junior High School.

In the futures courses which have been identified, student activities range from analyzing values to building dymaxion domes, from political action planning to science fiction reading and writing.

Study Materials

Among the systematic and comprehensive efforts to produce study materials for futures courses, *Worlds in the Making, Probes for Students of the Future* is a significant contribution. (3) In this book of readings the illustrated text introduces the many facets of futuristic thought to the high school student. The companion teacher's manual suggests activities which correlate with readings in the text.

The "View of the Twenty-first Century" syllabus, developed by Utica Free Academy staff and students, guided by Angela Elefante, provides another example of extensive effort and attention to detail. (4) Its assignments and readings, which are integrated into the manual, provide a one-volume introduction to study of the future.

Building the City of Man (5) (1971) is the first in a series of scholarly volumes produced by the World Order Models Project. The World Law Fund sponsors WOMP as one of its many educational projects directed toward world order. This book, indeed the entire WOMP series, provides substantive material for use in futures courses.

Special interest journals have devoted issues to futurism. The National Science Teachers Association, for example, published "To Invent the Future," a special issue of *The Science Teacher* (January, 1969). "Alternative Futures in Social Studies and Social Science Education" was a thematic issue of *The Social Science Record,* a journal of the New York State Council for the Social Studies (Spring, 1971). "Toward 2000 A.D.: Future Trends in Social Studies" was a feature of *The Social Studies Professional* newsletter of the National Council for the Social Studies (January, 1972). "The Future Is In Your Hands" was the theme of a recent issue of *Senior Scholastic,* a widely read student magazine for secondary school students. The theme was also extended to the complementary *Teacher's Education of Senior Scholastic* of the same date (April 24, 1972). In this manner, educators are being futurized through their specialized periodical literature.

The impact of a generally popular book, such as Alvin Toffler's *Future Shock* (1970), cannot be denied. (6) Not only do the publishers have trouble keeping up with the demand, but their offer of a free teacher's manual for the book was accepted by more than 43,000 who requested copies. (7) *Future Shock* is being used in elementary and secondary classrooms all over the nation. Certainly the wide acceptance of this book is an indicator of great public and school interest in futures literature. Jerome Agel authored the teacher's manual. No newcomer to the futuristic trade book scene, he has produced *U. S. History Not Taught in U. S. Schools* and *I Seem to be a Verb* (with R. Buckminster Fuller); *The Medium is the Massage,* and *War and Peace in the Global Village,* (with Marshall McLuhan) and many others. (8) All of these have been popular. As a futuristic communications specialist, Agel and his collaborators have tested the wind and found good weather.

Much earlier, R. Buckminster Fuller found wide acceptance of his sociotechnological futuristic ideas through *Nine Chains to the Moon* (1938). It is more popular now than when it was published. Fuller's recent books go through printing after printing. They include: *No More Secondhand God* (1963); *Operating Manual for Spaceship Earth* (1969); *Utopia or Oblivion Worldgame* (1969), and several volumes published by the World Resources Inventory Project in Carbondale, Illinois. Forward looking, forward thinking, "anticipatory design" oriented Fuller is a seminal thinker among futurists, an often used resource for the future studies teacher. (9)

Less well-known, but also futuristic and comprehensive in this thinking, is Julius Stulman, director of the World Institute Council and author of *Evolving Mankind's Future* (1967) and numerous other publications. (10)

Science fiction is an invaluable resource for the futures course. Many literature teachers have futurized their classes through science fiction reading and writing activities. The works of Arthur C. Clarke and Isaac Asimov are rarely absent from the futures teacher's reading list and book shelf.

The Year 2000 by Herman Kahn and Anthony J. Wiener (1967) (11) is an extensive introduction to futures projections. It remains a classic in the future study library, an example of scenario creation and an introduction to "Basic, Long-Term, Multi-fold Trends."

As an exemplar of the long-building concern in education with alternative futures, the early work of Theodore Brameld deserves acknowledgement. He directed a futures curriculum project during World War II in Floodwood, Minnesota, as reported in *Design for America: An Educational Exploration of the Future of Democracy for Senior High Schools and Junior Colleges* (Hinds, Heyden, and Eldredge, 1945).

⹀ An excellent bibliographic resource is the annual *Science for Society* bibliography issued at one dollar by the American Association of the Advancement of Science in Washington, D. C. The May 1972 edition lists 4000 futures or futures-related items, some with brief annotations. World Future Society president, Edward Cornish, has prepared a list of more than 100 futuristic films and their sources. Through the WFS headquarters in Washington, D. C., Cornish and staff publish *The Futurist,* provide a reader's service and a speaker's bureau, and coordinate World Future Society activities in major urban centers in the United States. They also coordinate international, national, and regional conferences of futurists. The film list is periodically updated. It and other WFS services are useful resources for the futuristic teacher and student.

Some Features of Futures Study

The unique feature of futuristic literature is not only its extensiveness but the interest which it has to the reader. It just might be that schools in this time period are in need of interesting reading materials in a wide range of formats and levels of difficulty. It just might be that futuristic ideas and materials could break through the motivation barrier by awakening interests dulled by an institutionalized fixation on the past.

Since future study incorporates data gathering and assessment of reality, secondary school students could be engaged in futuristic research projects using Delphi techniques for determining perceptions of probability and desirability. And many traditional techniques, such as interviewing and polling, can fit into a futuristic skill building framework.

Another feature of futures inquiry is its status equalization tendency. Since no one actually knows what the future will be like, it follows that students may inquire into the future as equals with their teachers. That is not to say that beginning students are equal in ability to experienced futures educators. It is to imply that the sorts of teachers who have become futures educators are not inclined to act in a superior status fashion in their interactions with students. The futures course provides, at least in the limited observations made, a receptive environment in which students and teachers inquire together into the unknown. This highly motivating, non-threatening relationship between futures teachers and students may merely reflect a selectivity. The teacher chooses the subject and the students choose both the subject and the particular teacher. A cadre can therefore be nurtured through which futuristic thinking and skills can be transferred to a wider range of students through, for example, peer teaching wherein students assist each other in learning. It is quite likely that whatever is done by a motivated minority, as in the futures class, will be heard about and sometimes transferred into the other classes in a school.

Toward a Clearinghouse

One lack, quickly evident in the investigation leading to this paper, was the absence of a clearinghouse for information and materials dealing with futurism in the schools. Respondents often asked questions about what is going on and who is doing what. To meet this perceived need, a Clearinghouse for Futuristic Studies in the Schools will offer services to inquirers who provide a self-addressed stamped envelope with inquiries directed to: CFSS, Social Studies Education, 412 Maxwell Hall, Syracuse University, Syracuse, New York 13210. If futurists in the schools will provide descriptions of their work, along with samples of the materials which are being used, futures information will be organized periodically and mailed to inquirers who have provided return envelopes. Primitive as this "shoestring" clearinghouse is, it can initiate a service which can be transferred when interest has grown and resources are available. Eventually, the ERIC system (Educational Resources Information Clearinghouse) may acknowledge future studies, as they have almost twenty other educational areas, and either create a Futures Clearinghouse or assign the area to an already established clearinghouse. For the time being, Clearinghouse for Futuristic Studies in the Schools will utilize the energies of futuristic college students and their professors in gathering materials and ideas and making these available at the lowest possible cost.

Futurism in the society is beginning to penetrate the schools. And though the field of future studies is immature, it is also substantive, open, and growing. There seems little doubt but that looking back from the year 2000, we shall regret some of the things we have done in futures education. But we will surely be glad that we started.

Notes

(1) See following essay by Michael Marien.
(2) Leon Festinger, Henry W. Riecken, and Stanley Schachter, *When Prophecy Fails, A Social and Psychological Study of a Modern Group that Predicted the Destruction of the World* (New York: Harper and Row, 1956).
(3) Mary Jane Dunstan and Patricia W. Garlan, *Worlds in the Making, Probes for Students of the Future* (Englewood Cliffs: Prentice-Hall, 1970).
(4) Angela Elefante et. al., *View of the Twenty-First Century, Syllabus for a Futures Course* (Utica, New York: Utica Free Academy, 1971). Correspondence can be directed to Dr. Angela Elefante, Federal-State Relations Office, 310 Bleecker Street, Utica, New York 13501.
(5) W. Warren Wager, *Building the City of Man: Outlines of a World Civilization* (New York: Grossman, 1971).
(6) Alvin Toffler, *Future Shock* (New York: Random House, 1970).
(7) Jerome Agel, *A Teacher's Guide to Future Shock* (New York: Bantam, 1971).

(8) Jerome Agel's futuristic books include *The Medium is the Massage* (New York: Bantam, 1967), *War and Peace in the Global Village* (New York: Bantam, 1968), *I Seem to be a Verb* (New York: Bantam, 1968), *The Making of Kubrick's 2001* (New York: New American Library, 1970), *The Radical Therapist, Volume One* (New York: Ballantine, 1971, *The Radical Therapist, Volume Two* (New York: Ballantine, 1972), *Is Today Tomorrow? A Synergistic Collage About Alternative Futures* (New York: Ballantine, 1972), *Herman Kahnsciousness* (New York: New American Library, 1972), *Understanding Understanding* (New York: Bantam, 1972) and *The Uncle Sam Papers* (in preparation).

(9) For an introduction to R. Buckminster Fuller's work, see Robert W. Marks (ed.), *Ideas and Integrities, A Spontaneous Autobiographical Disclosure* (Englewood Cliffs: Prentice Hall, 1963), and Robert W. Marks (ed.), *The Dymaxion World of Buckminster Fuller* (Carbondale: Southern Illinois University Press, 1960).

(10) Julius Stulman, *Evolving Mankind's Future* (Philadelphia: J. B. Lippincott, 1967). Stulman creates-writes-edits a periodical, *Fields Within Fields Within Fields*, published by the World Institute Council, 777 United Nations Plaza, New York, N. Y.

(11) Herman Kahn and Anthony J. Wiener, *The Year 2000: A Framework for Speculation on the Next Thirty-Three Years* (New York: Macmillan, 1967).

Part Five

The Future
of Educational Futures

XV

Toward
Linking Futurists
to the Academic World

Michael Marien

"Futures" is everywhere. It includes not only the work of those who call themselves futurists, but also all forms of futuristic expression—print and non-print, fictional and "factual," descriptive and prescriptive, academic and popular. The field is subject to many definitions; as defined here it encompasses any statement about trends (or what is changing), descriptive futures (or what might occur), prescriptive futures (or what ought to happen), and/or the methodology for making such statements. Although one does not have to be a futurist to make an important and plausible forecast or proposal for the future, those who concentrate on doing so are apt to be more successful. Given this bias, subsequent comments will be confined to describing the professional futurist, his work, and his relationship to other producers of knowledge.

High quality futures work, regardless of auspices, tends to be holistic and integrative, refining the best knowledge and opinion from everywhere and weaving it into illuminating combinations. The best futures literature presents alternatives, or, after having assessed the alternatives it suggests a single most probable and/or desirable path. From such literature, we can find positive visions to follow and negative visions to avoid or prepare for. By suggesting that which will be different in the future, empirical research in the present can potentially be guided to fresh sets of questions. (1)

So much for ideality. Much of the futures literature, especially in education, bears little resemblance to these criteria. Nearly all proposals are made without any consideration of alternatives or their consequences. The data base upon which one enters the future is often obsolete or inadequate. Many prescriptive futures reinvent old cliches—lifelong learning, open schools, human potentials—which may be necessary and desirable for the future, but are not distinguished from hundreds of similar statements. (2) Other exercises, such as enrollment forecasting. may become befuddled in the mechanics of ponderous methodology and emerge as scientistic trivia.

Also, there is a category of "non-futures futures" which may or may not be considered as within the field. These works of phony futurism, most notably associated with academic convocations and popular magazines, take advantage of some romantic sense of the future in their titling, but fail to provide any futuristic content. (3)

Thus, as in any discipline, there is high quality and low quality. The potential of educational futures to guide institutions and the learning of students within them can only be realized by identifying and promoting high quality work. To do so requires an appreciation of the relationship of futuristics to the existing body of knowledge and the relationship of futurists to other scholars in light of the conventions of knowledge production and dissemination.

A Taxonomy of Futurists

To understand the futurization of knowledge—how it is taking place and how it might best proceed—it is helpful to think of three ideal types of futurists: general futurists, specialized futurists, and futirized specialists. The key variables in this loose classification have to do with one's primary professional identity, the proportion of one's work that is futuristic, the scope of one's work, the sources on which it is based, and the audience at which it is aimed.

The general futurist is a full-timer, in touch with other general and specialized futurists. The general futurist calls himself a futures researcher, or a generalist. Or, he may employ a shifting set of multiple identities or eschew any description. In any event, he does not identify with any of the conventional, disciplines, professions, or problem areas. In this generalist mode, he serves as an integrator of knowledge, a coordinator among specialists, or an idea broker. He is apt to do work on forecasting methodologies that are applicable to many areas, and he is in an excellent position to serve as a critic.

The specialized futurist thinks of himself primarily as a futurist, but his work is generally confined to a single problem area such as education, the economy, or the impacts of new technology. He communicates with other futurists, as well as with specialists in his area of expertise. He is generally an outsider, though, lacking legitimacy or visibility among most of the specialists in his area of interest.

Because of the difficulties endemic in these futurist positions—general and specialized—the futurized specialist can play a critical role in brokering between futurists and non-futurized specialists.

The futurized specialist may or may not see himself as a futurist, but his primary identity is that of an economist, biologist, architect, or educator. He writes for his professional colleagues and not for futurists. Often, only part of his work can be considered as futuristic. Although it is broad in contrast to that of other specialists in his field, it is narrow in comparison with the work of specialized and general futurists. He may utilize the work of specialized futurists in his field, but he is generally unaware of the broader community of futurists and perhaps incapable of applying their work. For example, the architect as futurized specialist will investigate new building materials; as specialized futurist he relates the potential of these materials to social trends.

Unfortunately, most of the futures literature, as defined here, is the work of futurized specialists. Some of it is of high quality, but most of it is parochial. Therefore, it is desirable that the futurized specialist become aware of futurists and their work, not only as a means of extending his horizons vertically into the future and horizontally across problem areas and disciplines, but to further his critical role of professional leadership.

This simple taxonomy of general futurists, specialized futurists, and futurized specialists is proposed here as a means of understanding the futurization of knowledge and how it can be furthered. But there are other informing taxonomies. Elise Boulding, for example, discusses social planners, professional futurists (among which there are technocrats, humanists, and participatory futurists), social evolutionaires, ecological futurism, and revolutionary futurists (among which there are literary, political and social types). (4) Her outline suggests the ideological division among establishment technocrats, reformist humanists, and revolutionary radicals that is to be found in virtually every realm of thought.

Futuristics
and the Established Disciplines

There is a recurring question among futurists as to whether or not futuristics is a discipline, and, accordingly, whether the first priority is to establish a professional base or to futurize existing disciplines and professions.

It is convenient and conventional to think of every new grouping of scholars as a discipline, and to the extent that futurists meet together, (5) exchange papers, and publish journals, (6) they are acting as traditional scholars do. But futuristics is also a transdiscipline or a metadiscipline dependent on the work of many scholars in many fields. Further, the field incorporates a large body of work by those who do not and probably will not ever consider themselves to be "in" the field. And thus, if one sees futuristics as both a discipline and a transdiscipline, the answer concerning priorities is that there is an equal need to establish both a professional base and to consciously link up with all other areas of knowledge.

The organization of established scholarship, unlike that of futurists, consists of professional association that provides legitimacy, identity, and prestige on a national or global scale, in tandem with legitimate opportunities for employment in one's primary professional role. But employment for futurists *qua* futurists is largely confined to think tanks, (7) university-affiliated research institutes, and a few government agencies and corporations. There are virtually no positions for futurists in universities, although there are many futurists who are employed under conventional covers of political scientist, sociologist, etc. Consequently, a graduate student wishing to pursue study in futuristics must do so as a sideline to an established departmental program, but this can only be comfortably done under the aegis of one or more willing faculty. Given these constraints to the development of futurist manpower, it is notable that two "think tanks" (RAND and the Institute for Policy Studies) have recently established their own Ph.D. programs.

In the next few years, however, futurology programs at both graduate and undergraduate levels should proliferate even in the face of financial constraints. Concomitantly, the inexorable urge to legitimize will surely result in a professionalized association arising out of the International Futures Research Conference, the journal *Futures*, or the World Future Society (which at present is a semi-professional mixture of academics, students, bureaucrats, and other interested persons).

This is an important development, not only to students who wish to pursue integrative studies for pure or applied purposes, but also to society and its entire corpus of knowledge. Our knowledge remains severely fragmented into thousands of specialized areas that seldom benefit each other. A strong hub of integrative studies and knowledge brokering is necessary to correct the imbalance between specialists and generalists, adding coherence and perhaps even wisdom to what we know and what we seek to know. A professional society for futurists and opportunities for employment are necessary but insufficient steps for the futurization of knowledge. Futuristics as a transdiscipline is dependent on the knowledge base of established disciplines and in turn is potentially able to assist the disciplines in the pursuit of new knowledge.

It should be emphasized that many scholars will never develop their own futures perspective nor heed that of others—nor should they. But there are many others for whom a futures perspective could serve as a powerful aid to their work. Currently, the futurization of disciplines is the function of the futurized specialist. For example, in sociology, Wendell Bell and James A. Mau have recently edited *The*

Sociology of the Future (Russell Sage Foundation, 1971). In educational administration, the six members of the 1985 Committee of the National Conference of Professors of Educational Administration published *Educational Futurism 1985* (McCutcheon, 1971). A similar committee under the guidance of David Malcolm of the University of Pittsburgh, is planning a report on the implications of the future for educational counseling. The National Council of Teachers of English published a volume on futures in early 1972. In political science, Albert Somit is editing *Political Science and the Study of the Future,* and Magoroh Maruyama and James A. Dator have edited *Human Futuristics* as a result of a Symposium on Cultural Futurology held at the 1970 American Anthropological Society meeting. The 1971 meeting featured an Experimental Symposium on Cultural Futurology. In the hard sciences, Philip Handler has edited *Biology and the Future of Man* (Oxford, 1970), the distillation of 175 American scientists on 20 panels. In each of these instances, a book has been prepared by a futurized specialist—one who is interested in the future but whose primary professional identity remains as a sociologist, educator, counselor, political scientist, anthropologist, and biologist. And in each instance, the volume is addressed to professional colleagues by their respected peers. (8) The future relationship between futurized specialists and their colleagues within disciplines may very well parallel the relationship between futurists and futurized specialists. That is, there will be a recurring question as to whether the futurized specialist should integrate the sub-fields of his discipline or whether he should establish his own sub-field of sociological futuristics, educational futuristics, etc. It is probable that both lines of development will take place, leading to generalists and specialists within disciplines. Evidence of the latter development will emerge in several years with the appearance of a *Journal of Sociological Futures,* a *Journal of Educational Futures,* and other futures journals considered as sub-fields of established disciplines.

Futurists and Other Transdisciplines

Futuristics is only one of several foci for holistically organizing knowledge, and the recognition and ultimate interaction with other transdisciplinary movements is both necessary and desirable.

For instance, general systems theory is the study of the common properties of all systems—natural and man-made. General systems is not to be confused with systems analysis, which is often merely the systematic study of non-systems. The Society for General Systems Research has been convening since 1956, but there are no programs of study in general systems and only a few scattered courses. (9) On a pure-applied scale, the study of general systems tends toward the pure or non-applied end, although practical applications are not incompatible with this mode of thought. General systems is closely related to simulation (which can also be seen as a futurist methodology) and to cybernetics. Although there is little overlap at present between general systems and futuristics, the potential for a highly beneficial symbiosis is so great that some interplay between the fields would seem inevitable. Futuristics would benefit from the organizing focus afforded by systems theory; in turn, systems theory would benefit from greater attention to change processes and the positing of desirable system futures.

Policy Science is a new transdisciplinary area, defined by the journal *Policy Sciences,* first published in Spring 1970. Unlike general systems and futuristics, a formal association has yet to emerge, although there are already several graduate-level programs. These programs may not yet meet the ideal criteria that have been proposed; instead they may serve as a reshuffling of social scientists who genuinely wish to be relevant and/or make it in fat city. As outlined by Harold Lasswell who first proposed the concept of policy science in 1951, policy scientists should be problem-oriented as well as contextual, clarifying goals, viewing trends, utilizing scientific findings, projecting future possibilities and probabilities and inventing and evaluating alternative objectives and strategies:

The contemporary policy scientist perceives himself as an integrator of knowledge and action, hence as a specialist in eliciting and giving effect to all the rationality of which individuals and groups are capable at any given time. He is a mediator between those who specialize in specific areas of knowledge and those who make the commitments in public and private life (the public and civic order). (10)

Futuristics and policy science are quite obviously related. But there are differences: futures is more open to imagination (and sometimes flab), ideological prescription (and sometimes rhetoric), and alternative forms of presentation (and sometimes gimmicks). Policy science is potentially closer to the points of decision in high places, and more sober, hard-nosed, respectable. Yet, it is important that neither loses sight of the other: futuristics can add both creativity and long-term perspectives to policy science, which is subject to scientization and immediacy, whereas policy sciences can keep futuristics relevant to political realities and the needs of decision-makers.

There are two other transdisciplines that could be seen separately or as part of policy science: urban studies and ecology. Both provide visible and understandable justification for promoting general systems theory, futuristics, and policy science.

Each of these five transdisciplinary areas overlap each other to a considerable extent, and there are some individuals who contribute to several of them, while others identify with only one, either ignoring the other areas or perhaps presuming that their area has more "meta" than other meta-disciplines. (11) Each of these areas is ill-defined, with full-time and part-time contributors. And, most importantly, each area is subject to corruptive simplification of systems, futures, policies, urban areas and eco-systems, serving to compete with the quality work in each area. But each of these transdisciplines is a necessary intellectual adaptation to cope with the complexities that post-industrial man is creating. It is critically important that quality work in each area is promoted as quickly as possible.

Promoting Effective Futurization

Our static and atomized views of man, nature, and society have led to a perilous condition for humanity. Although estimates vary widely as to the grace period that separates us from nuclear holocaust, eco-catastrophe, widespread famine, or big brother control, it is increasingly recognized that new holistic cognitive styles are necessary to deal with our problems. Futuristics is one such style, and the ideas for its promotion are equally applicable to other transdisciplinary areas.

As previously mentioned, there is a need for both legitimate employment opportunities and for professional development. Both are necessary: without employment primarily as a futurist, the teacher and/or scholar will be forced to adhere to the standards of established disciplines; without professional development, there is little justification for employment.

Futurization is perhaps best promoted in schools and colleges by establishing a center or institute that interacts with other departments, rather than a conventional department that conducts its business in isolation from other departments. Or a futurist-in-residence program could follow the pattern of artist-in-residence or poet-in-residence that has been successfully employed in many institutions. One or more full-time futurists in every institution could work with various futurized specialists, helping them to broaden their interests and capacities to the fullest extent possible. Similarly, an opportunity for one or more general futuristics courses should be available to every student, and, for the many non-majors, every attempt should be made to relate general concerns for the future to the student's specific interests; that is, futures courses can and should interlock with most existing courses.

The necessary direction for professional development not only involves an association with meetings and journals, but also the identification of the vast futures literature that already exists and the development of a critical capacity. Wayne Boucher has conservatively estimated that there may be 50,000 futures-related books and articles in the English language alone, and, as societal transformation continues, the literature of trends, forecasts, and alternatives will continue to swell. But which among these many futures are to be taken seriously? Which are the exemplary statements—the visions that can guide us to a safe, just, and satisfying existence; the proposals, broad and narrow, that have been thought out as to secondary and tertiary consequences; the methods that can best enable us to investigate, and act wisely? And which visions in this century—and earlier—have proved essentially accurate, and why?

The difference between a profession and a mere movement is the identification of a body of literature, the capacity to select what is best from it, and an appreciation of the major visions of the past that might still have relevance to our future. Once these tasks are begun, futurists can then engage in a productive dialogue with traditional academics. For the futurization of knowledge, above all, has the potential to fruitfully integrate our understanding of the world and our search for further understanding.

Notes

(1) Several such exemplary books and articles are Peter F. Drucker, *The Age of Discontinuity* (New York: Harper & Row, 1969); Victor Ferkiss, *Technological Man* (New York: Braziller, 1969); Margaret Mead, *Culture and Commitment* (New York: Doubleday, 1970); W. Warren Wager, *Building the City of Man* (New York: Grossman, 1971), and John Platt, "What We Must Do" (*Science,* Nov. 28, 1969 pp. 1115-1121). An exemplary commission report with profound implications for education is the Sloan Commission on Cable Communications, *On the Cable: The Television of Abundance* (New York: McGraw-Hill, 1971). The most notable example of educational futurism is from a Swedish educator: Torsten Husen, *Present Trends and Future Developments in Education* (Toronto, Ontario Institute for Studies in Education, 1971). None of these documents, incidentally, employs "futures methodologies." Indeed, scientistic methodologies often inhibit a broad understanding of emerging realities.

(2) Michael Marien (comp.), *Alternative Futures for Learning: An Annotated Bibliography of Trends, Forecasts, and Proposals* (Syracuse: Educational Policy Research Center, May 1971).

(3) The most egregious example is Clarence W. Hunnicutt (ed.), *Education 2000 A.D.* (Syracuse: Syracuse University Press, 1956), reflecting many of the educational books of the fifties—and earlier—that use "future" in their titling without seriously considering a societal future other than the present. Some recent mis-titles include *Education: A New Era, Revoluation in Teaching, Educational Requirements for the 1970's,* and *Educating for the Twenty-First Century.*

(4) Elise Boulding, "Futuristics and the Imaging Capacity of the West," in Maroroh Maruhama and James A. Dator, eds., *Human Futuristics* (Honolulu: Social Science Research Institute, University of Hawaii, 1971) pp. 29-53.

(5) The First General Assembly of the World Future Society was held in Washington, D. C. in May 1971, while the first International Futures Research Conference was held in Oslo in 1967. In addition to these professional assemblages, more than 100 futures-related meetings have been held throughout the world, as reported in *Social Forecasting/Documentation 1971,* the futurist's global directory published by Instituto Ricerche Applicate Documentazione e Studi (IRADES) Via Paisiello 6, 00198 Rome, Italy.

(6) *The Futurist* has been published since 1967 and by the World Future Society; *Futures* since 1968 by Iliffe House in England; *Technological Forecasting* since 1969 by American Elsevier.

(7) Paul Dickson, *Think Tanks* (New York: Atheneum, 1971).

(8) In contrast, the volume that is most representative of professional futurists is Robert Jungk and Johan Galtung (eds.), *Mankind 2000* (London: Allen & Unwin, 1969), containing the proceedings of the above-mentioned Oslo conference. Especially see Edward S. Cornish, "The Professional Futurist" (pp. 244-250), which describes the role of general futurists employed by corporations.

(9) The Society has published the *General Systems Yearbook* since 1956 and will commence publication of the *Journal of General Systems* in 1972.

(10) Harold D. Lasswell, "The Emerging Conception of the Policy Sciences," *Policy Sciences,* 1:1 (Spring 1970), p. 13. Also see authoritative definitions by Erich Jantsch and Yehezkel Dror in the same issue.

(11) There are doubtlessly other new transdisciplines that claim a central position to all knowledge, (such as Ekistics: the science of human settlements) in addition to traditional disciplines such as philosophy, anthropology, politics (as originally construed), and history. Some of the best futurists come from these fields. Among the professions, journalism, politics, and the ministry each have an architectonic potential.